FROM STRENSALL TO SINGAPORE

A Personal Account of Service in
the Army and Royal Navy during
the Second World War

by
Harold Litchfield

Santona Publications
Hull

2

British Library Cataloguing-in-Publication data.
A catalogue record for this book is available from the British Library

Copyright © 1999 by Harold Litchfield and Santona Publications

First Published in 1999 on behalf of Harold Litchfield by;
Santona Publications
Rydal Mount
224 Marlborough Avenue
Hull HU5 3LE.

Design and typesetting by Santona Publications.
Printed by The Amadeus Press Huddersfield.

Harold Litchfield has asserted his rights under the Copyright, Design and
Patents Act 1988 to be identified as the author of this work.

ISBN 0 9507960 9 3

Foreword

Foot slogging with the Kings Own Yorkshire Light Infantry (160 paces to the minute) in the Army starting from Queen Elizabeth Barracks, Strensall in Yorkshire in 1940, to the Scottish borders with the 2nd/4th Battalion. Then back to Strensall, and then the invasion scare, when all forces were placed on full alert. Soldiers still in training, as well as those who had already seen service on the Continent, were waiting for the Germans to invade, which meant extra duties twenty-four hours a day. Training with the Scots Guards at Pirbright Signal Training Section and meeting up with their sturdy Sergeant Major, complete with measuring stick, and thence to the "Bow Bell" Division in London, Croydon Aerodrome and then to Holt in Norfolk from where I finally left, saying farewell to the Army, in December 1943.

I was to join a very different service life in the Royal Navy, sailing the high seas of the Atlantic, the Mediterranean and the far eastern waters to India and the then Dutch East Indies, Hong Kong and Malaya with a base at Singapore.

In January 1946, I returned on the battleship H.M.S. Howe to Portsmouth, the home port of Lord Nelson's flagship H.M.S. Victory, and received a hero's welcome home after six years of uncertainty, strife and stress; of not knowing what was going to happen from one day to the next. I had concluded six years of devoted service to King and Country.

This is not an account about feats of heroism, but about the everyday occurrences and duties performed by the average conscript in the last war. That's how it was fifty or more years ago and I was fortunate to be a survivor. Now read on.

Harold Litchfield
March 1999

DEDICATION.

I dedicate these memoirs to my late dear wife Doreen who died about two months before this manuscript was completed. She supported and encouraged me over a period of three to four years and read through the manuscript correcting where necessary.

She was a member of the Auxiliary Fire Service during the war. That battle she won, but unfortunately she lost her final battle against her illness.

God bless her and all the other countless service men and women who paid the supreme sacrifice with their lives in order that future generations may face a better future.

From Strensall to Singapore

CONTENTS

Part One. The Army Years

Chapter 1.

The Reason for Writing these Memoirs.

It is now fifty years or more since the end of the 1939-45 Second World War and since then some thousands of different volumes have been written about it. Prominent people, commanders in chief, government officials, war heroes in all the services, prisoners of war and individuals who felt that they had a story to tell.

In my particular case you might ask why I had waited fifty years to record my activities and participation in the war.

Well, the answer is that I managed to save a few photographs taken during my war service, particularly whilst in the Royal Navy, plus the fact that I kept a diary which was written in the last year of the war. In addition my family felt that it would be a good idea to record the information for future generations.

I found that there was a great deal of loyalty to the Crown during the Second World War, although reading about the First World War of 1914-18, I believe that the bond was even stronger then, and many more men and women gave their lives in that war. When I was a boy and although my father took part in the 1914-18 war, our family was reluctant to talk about it. My father did talk to me about his experiences and I have included some of them in with my own activities because there were some similarities to my own. My mother had her own thoughts on the subject but was very reluctant to discuss the war.

On reflection, between the older generation and the present younger generation the present day "troubles", I feel that we, as a nation, should have more discipline and that one way of achieving this is to have some form of National Service - not necessarily "square bashing"! The older generation will tell you that, in the case of school children, a certain amount of discipline with the use of a cane did them no harm but an awful lot of good.

I realise that unemployment plays a part in our troubles today, although incidentally the older generations had unemployment problems as well, but I still feel that emphasis should be placed on the control of families. Family units are nowadays constantly being split up (i.e. single parent families etc.) and this is where the damage is done. Also parents must accept more responsibility towards their children.

However, one must accept the fact that there is no easy solution to these kind of problems which do, after all, concern all of us as human beings.

Chapter 2.

My Family.

At the time of the commencement of the 1939-45 war I was a single person aged 19 years and it was not until after the war in 1954 that I married Hilda Doreen Pickersgill. We have two children, Rosalind and Martin George. Rosalind, the elder, is married to Steve and we have two grandchildren, two girls, Sarah Jane and Emma Kate. Martin is a bachelor and is pursuing his office career with a large firm dealing in heating boilers and radiators. He remains a bachelor, so he says, because he has seen so many of his friends get married and end up in the divorce courts. However time will tell as to whether he remains unattached. Martin is an enthusiastic Arsenal football supporter. Strange to relate that I also followed Arsenal when I was a schoolboy in the 1930s (like father like son?).

My wife Doreen (christened Hilda Doreen) whom I first met at my table tennis club served in the Auxiliary Fire Service during the war as a shorthand typist. During the war her home was bombed and badly damaged in the heavy air raid attacks on Hull and her family had to move into another house whilst repairs were carried out. Fortunately no one was seriously hurt.

Both my mother and father died some years ago. My mother died after a long illness which lasted some seven years. My parents came from different counties. My mother was from Lincolnshire (Scunthorpe) and my father was born in Leicester. I was one of three children, my brother Frank was the eldest, he was born during the First World War and my sister, who was the youngest, was born on Christmas Day 1920. Both my brother and sister were born in Lincolnshire and I was born near Patrington in the East Riding of Yorkshire on the 18th November 1919.

Sadly my brother Frank died suddenly at the early age of 63 years. He had served in the Royal Air Force, as a fitter on the ground staff, before the Second World War started. He was a motor mechanic in civilian life before joining up in 1937. Frank served at Biggin Hill during the "Battle of Britain" in September 1940 and later served abroad in Northern Rhodesia (now Zimbabwe), South Africa for

My Family.

Left to right; My mother, father, sister Doreen, myself and my brother Frank.

about 2 years. My father started work in Hull after he left the Hull Grammar School as a book-keeper and volunteered to serve in the 1914-18 war. In the year 1914, when his friends urged him to join up with them, he was offered a clerical post in the Lysaghts steel works in Scunthorpe which he accepted, so it was 1915 before he actually became involved in the First World War.

In that year (1915) he joined the 4th East Yorkshire Regiment which at that time had its training headquarters at Dalton Holme, near Beverley in the East Riding of Yorkshire. He was sent to France in 1917 and took part in the Battle of the Somme and managed to survive the last year of the war in 1918.

During the 1939-45 war my father was in the Civil Service in the County Court. At the outbreak of the war in September 1939 he was transferred to the local Ministry of Transport for the duration of the war and was responsible, amongst other things, for the requisitioning of vehicles into government service to help the war effort.

My sister Doreen volunteered and joined the A.T.S. serving in the cipher section in this country and was later transferred to Belfast where she met, and eventually married, a leading hand in the Royal Navy, Edmund Carroll (later to become a petty officer). She was married in Hull on the 30th September 1944. Unfortunately I was the only one in our family who was unable to attend her wedding because I was serving in the Royal Navy in the Mediterranean at that time. Her husband Edmund was in the peace time Royal Navy and saw service both in home waters and abroad, including the Mediterranean and the East Indies. During this time he was torpedoed twice but managed to survive to tell the tale. At the end of the war he continued to serve in the Navy for a period of time, before returning to civilian life once more. My sister Doreen has four children; John, Gerald, Pamela and Geoffrey, and four grand children.

As far as my own career was concerned I left Riley High School in 1935 and my father and I decided that I should attend the Hull College of Commerce which would help me to find better employment in the commercial sector. So I took a one year course in typewriting, book-keeping and accounts.

After leaving the Hull College of Commerce I managed to get a position as a junior typist with a local firm of solicitors, but I really wanted to get into accountancy if possible. After three months with the firm of solicitors, a vacancy arose with a firm of Incorporated Accountants (a one man business) and so I joined them as a junior clerk. One of the accountants senior male employees was a German who had emigrated from Germany well before the First World War and he was a volunteer for this country in the 1914-18 war. Unfortunately he lost part of one of his legs and had to use crutches for walking. He was very fearful of the Nazis and was appalled at the way they were treating the Jewish people in Germany and elsewhere. He told me that he thought that Germany would not be deterred from their aggressive intentions. I had the same opinion at the time, and in fact we were given a year's grace from 1938 until September 1939.

My grandfather Walter Litchfield lived in Leicester before coming to Hull in the late eighteen hundreds. His ancestors came from a

Walter Litchfield J.P.
Grandad
1866 - 1932

small village about eight miles north of Bedford called Risley and when I was a boy I had the pleasure of visiting the village whilst on a cycle tour with my father. We visited the village church yard and saw the graves of my grandfather's ancestors. His mother was named "King" and his father was a "Litchfield". In fact the church yard contained many graves with the two names. My father and I spoke with some of the "Litchfields" in the village and met one of the oldest of them, an "Uncle Eli" who was ninety years old and still quite active.

My grandfather became a Justice of the Peace when he lived in Newstead Street, Hull and was an active member of the Labour Party in Hull in the late twenties and early thirties. He was also a Hull councillor representing the Labour Party. He was also chairman of the Hull Co-operative Society's Education Committee at the time of his death in 1932.

When he first came to Hull he set up in business as a rully builder, which were horse drawn, and he had the order to build rullies used by the Hull Co-operative Society at that time before the days of motor vehicles. However, as we became "motorised" he eventually had to give up the rully business. He was also the editor of the "Wheatsheaf " for a number of years, the official monthly journal of the Kingston Upon Hull Co-operative Society Ltd. In addition he was quite a good artist, particularly in oil painting, and he had his portrait of a Bedfordshire Lace Maker shown in the Ferens Art Gallery in Hull. A number of portraits of my father in his First World War uniform in the East Yorkshire Regiment were also part of his work. His hobby, apart from painting, was gardening and he had an allotment in Perth Street which included a greenhouse and his speciality was the "passion flower".

The following chapters tell of my own involvement in the Second World War, of the tragedies and of the living from one day to another without knowing what was in store in the future.

Chapter 3.

Army Life - 1940 to 1943
Queen Elizabeth Barracks, Strensall near York.

The war scare started in September 1938 when Adolf Hitler threatened to take over more countries occupied by Germans. Mr Chamberlain, then the Prime Minister, went to Munich to attend a meeting of various Heads of State. He returned from that meeting stepping off the plane in this country waving a piece of paper saying, "I have here a piece of paper signed by Adolf Hitler himself stating that there will be no war between this country and Germany." Twelve months later we were at war with Germany, so much for the signed piece of paper. Most people believed in 1938 that war would come in the near future. The twelve month's grace gave us some time to build up our defences. However Germany had been doing this for many years.

I received my calling up papers in November 1939 and had to attend at the local army barracks for medical checks etc. I was asked which service I would prefer to join and I stated a preference for the Royal Air Force because my brother Frank was already serving as a fitter on the ground staff. I was told that they needed infantry men, and so that was that, I would join the infantry. When one volunteered, or was conscripted into the Army, you always went to the allotted camp early on the Friday morning in order that you had a week-end to settle in; and so it was for me.

It was an emotional time having to leave the family for the first time, leaving early that morning. I had to report to the Paragon railway station in Hull where the recruits assembled, then we were ushered on to trains heading for York. I remember that it was the middle of February and the weather was quite cold with a covering of snow on the ground at the time. On arrival at York railway station there was a number of army lorries (2 tonners) all lined up outside the station waiting to transport the recruits, including myself, to Strensall camp about seven miles outside York.

So it was that I joined the Kings Own Yorkshire Light Infantry at their training centre at Strensall on the 15th February 1940. My father had been a signalman in the 1914-18 war serving with the 4th

New recruit Pte H. Litchfield
No 4693517. Queen Elizabeth Barracks, Strensall near York.
February 1940.

East Yorkshire Regiment and he spent some time in the trenches in 1916 dodging the German shells. He had told me how, when he joined up, everyone believed that the war which started on the 4th August 1914 would be over by Christmas that year. How wrong they were. When I joined up in February 1940 I knew that the war was not going to end after a short time.

Going to war was a strange and new experience for a young person, one's life was going to change completely and so it was. Before going into the army I was training to become an Incorporated Accountant (since merged with the Chartered Accountants) and I was employed in office work, book-keeping, typewriting etc, a nine-to-five job. Army life as a recruit was very different.

On my first day in the army (recruits always started on a Friday) you were given your inoculations to protect you against various diseases. You had just the week-end to get ready to start your training in earnest early on Monday morning. Reveille was at six thirty, you got up, washed and shaved, made your bed and went for breakfast at seven o'clock .You started your training after breakfast at 8.30 a.m. Lunch was usually around midday and tea at 4.50 p.m. Infantry training consisted of a great deal of marching, drill, etc. The light infantry marching pace was the quickest in the British Army, one hundred and sixty paces to the minute. There was rifle drill, weapon training, field craft, shooting on the rifle ranges, current affairs. Whilst in early training, one of the main activities was "Kit Inspection". The idea was to check that each recruit had a full set of equipment. These inspections were ordered from time to time. When one occurred, you had to set out on your bed in neat lines your personal kit; i.e. knife, fork and spoons, mess tin, spare socks, field dressing, spare underwear, etc., rifle pull-through (used to clean your rifle), blankets and various bits and pieces including cleaning materials. Another chore that you had to do was to ensure that your army boots were always clean on special parades, including the commanding officer's weekly parade in the main barrack square. This was when your boots had to really shine with a great deal of "spit and polish", otherwise you were in trouble.

New recruits Pte Hamblett & Pte Litchfield.
Queen Elizabeth Barracks, Strensall near York.
February 1940.
Pte Hamblett from Halifax had both his legs blown off by a
mine whilst serving with the K.O.Y.L.I. in Italy in 1944. The
hospital authorities managed to save his life

We also had regular rifle inspections, this was to ensure that your rifle was always clean and in good working order, we also had inspections after we had used our rifles on the firing range. This entailed pouring boiling water down the barrels after firing and cleaning the barrel with a rifle pull-through which contained a piece of cleaning rag with a little oil on it.

It was like being at school again, you had a set programme each day Monday to Friday with the commanding officer's parade on a Saturday morning. You had church parade on Sunday morning if you were not on a week-end pass. In addition, recruits had to take their turn with guard duties. This entailed guarding prisoners which were called "defaulters". The duty usually started at 7 p.m. and you came off duty at seven in the morning. Your hours of duty depended on the number of men detailed for guard duty that day. My turn came for guard duty one summer evening. On this particular night, three of us were on duty at the same time at 2 a.m., guarding the guard room itself and the adjoining cells. One of the prisoners decided to escape whilst the three of us were on duty. Unfortunately, none of us saw him escape, consequently the three of us were placed on a charge and had to appear before the commanding officer for allowing the prisoner to escape.

Fortunately, the prisoner who had escaped had been recaptured before he'd got very far away from the camp, plus the fact that the average age of the three of us was only 19, the commanding officer took a lenient attitude. Our punishment was that we were confined to barracks for seven days.

We were billeted in wooden huts which usually had beds for about 30 men and a corporal. During my first spell of training, one of the recruits had loaded his rifle in one of the huts, stood the rifle near his head, pulled the trigger, that was the end of him. He was given a full military funeral and I was detailed as one of the coffin bearers.

When I first started my initial infantry training it was winter time and we used to use Strensall Common for quite a lot of our training. At that time of the year the ground was wet and boggy with quite a lot of water about. This was the area that we did our field craft training involving crawling about on the grass with our rifles at the ready. I believe that this was the cause of me becoming ill with pneumonia. I remember when I was first wheeled into Clifton hospital from the Army truck which brought me from the barracks' sick bay. One of the young trainees said to one of the other nurses. "He (meaning me) looks very still, I wonder if he is paralysed." I was amused by the remark because, of course, I was not paralysed. Strange to relate I was in more pain whilst in the sick bay for two days before the medical officer decided to send me to hospital. Whilst I was in hospital the Princess Royal visited the patients. I was given treatment with M & B Tablets, the treatment seemed to work very well because I was only in the hospital for ten days. I remember at the time lying in bed and listening to Judy Garland singing the song "Over The Rainbow" on the hospital radio, that was one of the popular songs of the day. I left the Clifton hospital after ten days and was only granted seven days sick leave.

I remember that in May 1940 whilst on sick leave the weather was really hot and sunny. It was times like that which made you homesick. After sick leave I returned once again to Strensall and continued my training. It was during this time, June 1940, that the retreat from Dunkirk took place. As a result of the retreat, all military personnel were confined to barracks for some considerable time. It was thought by the high command that the Germans might be planning to invade the country. Because of this all available troops (including those still training) were used to guard our aerodromes. This order gave us extra training duties, we still did our training during the day, but after tea we had to dress in full marching order and proceed to one of the local aerodromes where we had to stand guard around the airfield until the early hours of the morning awaiting a possible invasion. It was an unusual experience stood there in the open fields with your rifle at the ready waiting silently for the enemy to arrive.

At this time when invasion by the Germans was a possibility, more emphasis in our training was put on small arms drill and fire, getting used to rapid fire. As a result of this thinking quite a number of targets in the form of a bulls eye were painted on the walls of the barracks and after each days normal training the platoon would assemble lying down on the ground in front of the various targets and the N.C.O.s would conduct a number of rapid fire exercises at the targets. Of course no live ammunition was used.

This sort of training was the order of the day for the remainder of the time that I was at Strensall. The aerodrome patrols went on for quite a while. We now know that at that particular time no attempt was made to invade this country. Adolf Hitler had other ideas.

During our early training a most important item on our programme was route marching. For these marches we were usually dressed in full marching order with rifles slung. The distance varied, we started off with five mile marches and these were increased over a period of time. On some occasions the regimental band would head the march and we always sang the popular songs of the day as we marched along; "Roll Out The Barrel", "We'll Meet Again", "I've Got Sixpence", etc. It was essential when training with the army (especially in the infantry) to keep oneself fit - route marching helped but, oh, those sore heels! Our instructors used to say; "It is you or Gerry (meaning the Germans) who will survive," so you had to make sure that you were fit. It was in your interest in order to survive. After the normal route marches came; "The run a mile" and "March for Two", this sorted out the men from the boys.

Around late September, early October 1940, came a pleasant surprise in our army training at Strensall. Quite a number of recruits including myself were to help in the potato harvest in Lincolnshire. A train load of recruits from Strensall left the station with the sole purpose of providing casual labour in the potato fields. We were taken to Grantham railway station where we left the train and paraded on the station ready to march off to some temporary billets. These were not far from the fields where we were to do our "Potato Picking". Our job consisted of picking up the potatoes from the soil and placing them in baskets. This was after the farmer had harvested them from the ground. We would leave the billet by army truck about 9 a.m. each morning to be taken to the various fields. About 20 to 30 recruits would be allocated to each field. Then the party would be split up into "Working Lines".

Then the picking would commence with a break at lunch time, then we would continue until about 4 o'clock in the afternoon. Usually the farmer would provide sandwiches at the lunch break. At the end of each day we would line up in the field and the farmer would stand there with a bag of half crowns. Each soldier received one half crown for a hard days work, which was back breaking too. We worked in the fields for one week after which time some other troops took over and we returned by train to Strensall.

I remember one day the farmer set us working in the morning and we did not see him again all day. The consequence was that we had no lunch and we were really hungry at the end of the working day. In fact we were so hungry that most of us took some of the potatoes, cut them and peeled them with a knife that we had with us and sat down and ate them raw. They tasted good because we were so hungry. Also we did not get our half crowns either, we reported the fact later but nothing came of it, we in fact did a hard days work with no reward.

Although this exercise was different, I think the majority of us were glad to get back to the usual training routine. Before leaving this subject there was also a humorous side to the business of "Potato Picking". One of our colleagues working in our line was not too keen on the job, so what he did was to put one or two potatoes in the basket and the third one he would put his foot on and the potato was buried back in the ground, he then shouted out "next year". And so he went on, putting two in the basket and burying the third one back in the soil. I suppose it was his way of objecting to the job. It was very amusing at the time to the rest of us in the line, but I don't suppose the farmer would be very pleased. No doubt the farmer raked the field later for the odd potatoes.

Chapter 4.

Hawick, Scotland.

After intensive training at Strensall the 2nd/4th Battalion of the Kings Own Yorkshire Light Infantry, of which I became a member together with other recruits, was to leave bound for Scotland and Stobbs Camp near Hawick. We left Strensall railway station and proceeded to Manchester where we were to stay for two days and nights at a transit camp next to the Manchester railway station before making our way up north to Stobbs Camp. The transit camp turned out to be part of the Manchester Zoo and Speedway Arena. It was very strange to get out of your bed in the morning and within a few yards of your billet you could gaze on all kinds of different animals large and small including lions and tigers. On the first night we were allowed out of camp but we had to don full marching order (equipment-wise) together with our rifles including a bandoleer of ammunition ready for action in case of an invasion emergency. I remember going to sit in a cinema in Manchester that night with my rifle by my side together with my bandoleer of ammunition. The film being shown was the well known "Gone with the Wind" starring Clark Gable. It was quite a long film and because of the limited amount of time allowed away from the camp I was not able to see all of the film. However you had to make the most of your free time in the army.

On the second night I thought I would visit the speedway track next to the billet and I saw some exciting races. In one particular race one of the riders was thrown over the motor cycle's handlebars, and was badly injured. I suppose it can be a dangerous sport. After assembling the following morning back at Manchester railway station our next stage in the journey was to proceed by rail to Stobbs Camp near Hawick.

We were to be under canvas and I understand that the camp was used during the 1914-18 war. It transpired that the battalion was to train in Scotland for special duties. Our training consisted of route marching in hilly terrain with special emphasis on physical fitness. We were not told at this stage what we were supposed to be training for, however, I was soon to leave the battalion. Before leaving I was able to explore the surroundings of the camp and not far away was a small woollen factory and looking through the windows of the building you could see the wool machines spinning the different coloured wools into pattern. Of course the area was always well known for the processing of wool and today there is still quite a number of mills in the area.

After about four or five weeks training I was again hospitalised. This time with a whitlow on my right thumb which became poisoned, causing my thumb to swell to about three times its normal size. The cause was attributed to some dirt getting into my thumb whilst digging trenches around the camp when we first arrived. After attending the sick bay for a few days the medical officer decided that I needed hospital treatment, so I was taken to the nearest military hospital, which was in Galashiels. It was now November 1940 and I unfortunately had to spend my 21st birthday in hospital, however all was not "doom and gloom" because I received by post from my mother and aunt Aggie two nice home made fruit cakes which went down very well.

My poisoned thumb would not heal in spite of the fact that I had three operations on it, including one to remove part of the bone that had been infected. The nurses and staff were very good to me and I had no cause for complaint. I was also thankful for the fact that if I was not in hospital I could have been in some other theatre of war.

One thing that was new to me was eating porridge with salt, I had always had porridge at home with sugar.

After about two months my thumb began to respond to treatment and it began to heal. This was good news for me because I was allowed out in the hospital grounds and I became part of the now "walking wounded". During one of my short outings I met a farmer ploughing a field nearby and he called to me and asked me which regiment I belonged. I told him it was K.O.Y.L.I. whereupon he replied that he was in the same regiment in the First World War! It is indeed a small world.

On another occasion I walked into Galashiels, which was not very far from the hospital, and I had a look at some of the shops in the town. I managed to buy one or two souvenirs including for my mother, a metal tray portraying Abbotsford House, Galashiels, the home of Sir Walter Scott. There was a library there which contained 9000 books, an armour collection, historical relics and paintings. On another afternoon during my convalescence I was walking along the Tweed valley and saw a group of Scottish pipers in their kilts in the distant hillside playing some of the Scottish tunes. It was a sight to remember.

Whilst in hospital we (the patients) often received visits from local people bringing to the hospital "Comforts for the Forces" which consisted mainly of knitted goods, gloves, mittens, stockings and balaclavas etc. When this happened the various items would be shared amongst the patients and, I remember, I did receive a pair of mittens on one occasion which was very much appreciated.

Christmas day came along and I was still in hospital. The routine in a military hospital did not change even at Christmas. However, we did know that it was Christmas day because each patient who wanted one was given a pint of beer, well done the Scots! I do not usually drink beer but I had a pint on this occasion and really enjoyed it; perhaps it was because it was Christmas.

Early in the new year (1941) I remember we had a scattering of snow on the hills around the hospital. Whilst in the hospital at Galashiels I became friendly with one of the young nurses called Esther who lived in Galashiels. She gave me her address when I left hospital. I did correspond with her for a short time. Her father had a greengrocer's shop in Galashiels. However the friendship did not last long and I did not see her again. It was now February and the Scottish countryside was beginning to look spring-like with early violets and primroses; the scenery was really pleasing to the eye. One good thing about the war was that it made one aware of the wonders of nature in troubled times.

The time had come in February 1941 for me to leave hospital where I had spent the last three months. My thumb had now healed up and after saying my farewells and thanks to the staff it was time for me to return once more to the infantry training centre at Strensall. Shortly after arriving back in Strensall in 1941, Hull, my home town suffered some of the worst bombing raids from German aircraft. Hull was always referred to as "A North Eastern Town".

Because of the continuous raids and the lack of sleep my Mother fell down the stairs and broke both her arms. Fortunately I was able to obtain 48 hours compassionate leave from the camp at Strensall. Eventually her arms healed and were back in use again, but those sort of injuries take time to heal completely. My father was at home and he was able to take care of her. I was glad of the opportunity to see my mother, but 48 hours (including travelling time) does not give one enough time at home.

With regard to my stay in hospital, I did learn towards the end of the war from a colleague who was in the 2nd/4th Battalion K.O.Y.L.I., that the battalion that I had left behind when I went into hospital had gone abroad shortly afterwards. I learned that only one third of the battalion returned to this country and that the rest had either been killed or taken prisoner.

You could say that going into hospital may have saved my life. It was in fact a case of history repeating itself. My father experienced some lucky escapes during the First World War. On one occasion whilst serving with his signal platoon (he served in the East Yorkshire Regiment) he was one of a number of signalmen allocated to different companies, he came back to headquarters but others did not.

On another occasion whilst in the trenches he was hit by shrapnel in his back, but fortunately for him he was a keen reader and always kept some books in his pack on his back. The shrapnel lodged in his books and not in his back, a kind of hidden armour.

Chapter 5.

Dursley, Gloucestershire.

I arrived back once again in Strensall and went back to the usual infantry training which by now had been brought more up to date as the months went by. However after a further period of training it was decided in view of the threat of invasion, to form a defence battalion and I was part of the battalion which was to be sent to Dursley in Gloucestershire in February 1942.

So once again I was to leave Strensall. We established a camp on the outskirts of the village which was about five miles from Stroud, a larger village. The village itself was ideal for street fighting training and on the outskirts there were plenty of green fields and open countryside. The emphasis was on field training and open warfare as well as battalion manoeuvres. In view of the fact that this battalion was formed as part of the defence of the realm we had two officers who were veterans of the First World War.

Whilst in Dursley use was made of the local conditions which were ideal for battalion manoeuvres and a great deal of emphasis was placed on this type of training. The main street ran in a sort of valley which was good for mock battles etc. Fortunately 1942 was a good sunny summer during our stay at Dursley. When we had any free time we used to visit Stroud which was larger than Dursley. To get there you could either take a bus or train. Since this was only a branch line a very small engine was used to haul the carriages. The little engine was known as "The Dursley Donkey". The train journey was about three miles and only took a short while. Whilst I was stationed at Dursley I was fortunate enough to meet an N.C.O. in the K.O.Y.L.I., (not our battalion) who was working in the company office of another battalion. He was Lance Corporal Cyril Finch and he came from my home town of Hull. He was an insurance agent in civilian life and I was able to meet him once again after the war whilst cycling in the town. However I have lost touch with him since.

Whilst in Dursley I had my photograph taken with some of the service personnel including Cyril Finch and an R.A.F. man. I managed to get a copy of the photograph which I still have today. In our free

Dursley, Gloucestershire.

Taken near the Toc H Canteen in Dursley, Gloucestershire.
Centre back L/Cp. Finch from Hull, myself on the right

time, mainly weekends we used to explore the surrounding
countryside. There was a point in the hills where it was possible to
see a number of different counties at the same time. The hill was
called "Stinchcombe". A few miles away was another high point

called "Nibley Knoll". On a clear day you could see the River Severn as well as two other Counties; Avon and Wiltshire.

Whilst on the subject of the town of Dursley, on the outskirts of the town was a factory that made metal waste bins used in public places and gardens and I understand that these bins are still being produced today. We used to march by the Factory on our way to daily exercises and manoeuvres.

I liked Stroud because there was a Y.M.C.A. in the town which had a table tennis table and I always enjoyed a good game of table tennis, provided that I could find a partner who was willing to take me on. Whilst in the army I found that many Y.M.C.A.s and Toc H.s usually had a table tennis table in their canteens which was most helpful. I found that a good game was very relaxing since it was my favourite sport at that time, and still is. Sometimes I could persuade some of my colleagues in the signal platoon to give me a game, and one of my best opponents was a Jewish man called Silverman who came from London and during the time that he was with the platoon we enjoyed some good games. He won some and I won some. I remember that when he was feeling good he would sing the well known song called "Stardust". Incidentally he volunteered for overseas service and I had the good fortune to meet him later. This came about when I was in the Royal Navy in Naples Bay for a short while and he was stationed near Naples with a K.O.Y.L.I. battalion serving in Italy. We only had a short time to talk and naturally we searched for a table tennis sports hall in Naples. We found one, but all the tables were fully booked so we did not get a game after all.

In most of the Y.M.C.A.s and canteens there was usually a piano, and there was always someone who could "Tickle the Ivories" playing all the modern songs of the day and many service men and women could give a rendering of classical music. Whilst in the army I was never fortunate enough to be at a camp where one was entertained by professional entertainers such as ENSA, although I must say they did a good job as far as entertaining the troops was concerned.

Chapter 6.

Chilbolton, Hampshire and
The Scots Guards Training Course, Pirbright.

After three or four months training at Dursley the battalion moved further south to a small village called Chilbolton, which was in Hampshire. The camp itself was in a small wood with quite a number of grey squirrels in the trees. The billets consisted of a number of large round aluminium huts. Our training was very similar to that at Dursley but the emphasis was more on long route marches which we made in the area.

I remember that we could not leave any food, sweets or chocolates near the beds in the billet otherwise they would be eaten by field mice since the billet was in fact in a wood. The nearest town of any size was Winchester, which is famous for its cathedral with a very long nave, this was about a five mile walk from the camp. During our time off I was able to visit the cathedral and I was surprised at the amount of history which can be seen in the building.

The battalion had only been at Chilbolton for a few weeks when it was decided that our signal platoon should be sent on a four week signal course, myself included, and we were to be attached to the Scots Guards training centre at Pirbright, the home of all the guard regiments. The camp is in a wooded and hilly area and was well suited for signal training, which included the use of semaphore flags and lamp signalling. The No 18 wireless sets were now being issued by signal platoons for use in the field which led to better and more modern communications. Although we were on a signal course, we still had to do some "Square Bashing" which meant marching on the Guards' parade ground. We would fall in at the rear of the Scots Guards and the Guards' sergeant major, with his measuring stick, would watch the parade.

He would find fault with our marching with such remarks as (addressing one of us) "What's your number?" (meaning regimental number). On giving the number the sergeant major would say, "Great Scot," or words to that effect (they were Scots Guards after all). "Your number isn't dry yet!" (meaning that we were not old hands).

The discipline in the Guards was of a very high standard and whilst you were in their barracks you had to adhere to their rules and regulations. Incidentally the measuring stick was used to measure one's steps when marching which should be a certain distance apart, that is for guardsmen. An example of the strict discipline occurred one evening in the barrack room when sergeant instructors were not allowed in other ranks' barrack rooms (except on duty of course) and in this instance one of the sergeants was chatting when the orderly officer was doing his rounds. As soon as the sergeant heard the orderly officer approaching he leapt through one of the open windows in the room (James Bond style), the window being on the ground floor, thus avoiding the officer. A close shave?

Whilst on the course we used to have morning and afternoon breaks in the training grounds where a mobile canteen was manned by a 1914-18 war veteran who had a bar of medals handy for when any army officers were around. When they arrived on the scene the veteran would clip his row of war medals on to his coat and when they had gone, he would take them off again.

Our signal training course consisted of a mixture of marching on the parade ground and signal training using semaphore flags, lamps and lastly but most important of all, we used the No. 18 wireless set which was the new addition to the infantryman's means of communication. The terrain around the camp was ideal for operating lamps and semaphore work; the training area was hilly and very wooded. At the conclusion of the course we had to do various tests in sending and receiving messages.

We were tested in the different methods of communication, but we did not have an examination test. Throughout the course we all found the Scots Guards instructors very co-operative and everyone got on well with them. Whilst we were on the signal course at the Guards depot we had to take our turn of "Policing Duties" on Woking railway station which was only a short distance from the camp.

I remember that we worked in twos and we were issued with special helmets. Our job was to supplement the "Red Caps" and help to keep law and order on the railway station. I remember that we did a three hour stretch of duty on one particular night. The railway station was very busy indeed with service personnel coming and going but we did not have any trouble to deal with whilst on duty.

Now that we had completed our signal course it was back once again to Chilbolton and the wooded camp with the grey squirrels. It was whilst we were stationed at Chilbolton that the battalion was taken in army trucks to Poole in Dorset to take part in an exercise involving infantrymen advancing under fire with cover being provided by twenty-five pounder Royal Artillery guns.

The exercise took place on a special army training area used for this type of special training. The area was very hilly and the Royal Artillery guns were lined up at the foot of a hill and we, the infantrymen, were formed into sections and then ordered to advance up this hilly section for about a mile. The Royal Artillery guns would open up and fire over our heads. The exercise lasted about two hours and of course as long as the guns were accurate, we had nothing to worry about. However there were no accidents and the experience was very valuable from our point of view. It proved to be another different days work for us, and so we returned once again to our base at Chilbolton.

Chapter 7.

Croydon.

Our next move as a defensive battalion was to Croydon during the Summer of 1942 where we became part of the "Bow Bells" division in the London area. Our battalion was billeted in requisitioned houses and this time our job was to defend Croydon aerodrome. Our daily programme always started early in the morning with a physical training session and a run round the houses in the area. I remember that, apart from the actual patrols around the aerodrome, we had route marches from time to time. The actual patrol around the perimeter of the aerodrome was worked on a rota basis. Croydon at the time was a very busy military aerodrome and there was always plenty to see when on patrol. During our time off we used to go for walks on Croydon Common a large open pleasant park area.

It was during this term of duty that I met a girl from Croydon; Miss Hilda Howe. She was a factory worker in a local munitions works. We met on several occasions and I was invited to tea once or twice at her home in Croydon which made a nice change from army routine. The family were very good to me, her father was an inspector of taxes and her mother was kind and understanding. Hilda also had a younger sister who was still at school. Whilst at Croydon I obtained a 48 hour pass and I asked Hilda if she would like to accompany me home and she was glad to have the opportunity to see what life was like in a northern town. I think she preferred the south, but enjoyed the visit. When I left the area I still communicated with her by letter and we remained good friends for a number of years. I did not learn later whether or not she eventually got married.

During this time our signal sergeant (Sergeant Jewson) used to give lectures on signal procedures to the Home Guard personnel in the locality after training hours.

The driver of the signal platoon's 15 cwt truck, Bill Herbert, used to take me with him in the truck (with the sergeant's permission) and we enjoyed a few evenings in the local pub whilst the sergeant was giving his lectures. Needless to say he would join us later before we made our way back to the camp. It was during some of these sessions that I was given an opportunity to learn to drive the 15 cwt truck, which was unofficial, since at that time I did not have a driving licence. However the experience, although somewhat limited, did help me in later life with my car driving. Of course in the case of the army truck it was all "double de-clutching", but not so for driving cars.

One good thing about being billeted in Croydon was that it gave us easy and quick access to the capital, although in 1942, air raids were quite frequent and I witnessed quite a lot of air raid damage in the streets of London. I found that the people were very resilient indeed and they carried on with their daily lives regardless. It was during my stay at this billet that I became the quartermaster sergeant's assistant for one week whilst the regular assistant went on leave. It was a question of doing yet another different kind of duty in the army which I quite enjoyed. My main task was checking the various items of different stores kept by the quartermaster. Everything had to be listed and every little item had to be accounted for, which was typical of army routine. His stores even included condoms which in those days were referred to as "French Letters". At the end of each day I had to do a reconciliation showing what goods had been received and those that had been issued. Also at the end of the week I had the job of sorting out the weeks movement of stores and reconcile the figures with the actual stocks remaining.

It was certainly a different routine and I enjoyed the change but I was glad to get back to the signal platoon.

With regard to the air raids on London, the capital was now bombed by the new German bomb, the Vl rocket, to be followed by the bigger and more dangerous bomb the V2. Whilst in Croydon, and on my trips to the capital, I saw quite a lot of the damage done by these new bombs. The craters were much bigger and covered a much larger area than the conventional bombs used previously. I remember walking around London during my time off and was surprised by the extent of the damage, however, St. Paul's Cathedral managed to get away with only minor damage.

It was now Autumn and our term of duty at Croydon came to an end. The battalion returned once again to base at Strensall. Within a short time of arriving back we were ordered to Scotland.

Chapter 8.

St. Andrews, Scotland.

It was October 1942 and this time our destination was St. Andrews on the east coast of Scotland. We left Strensall, the infantry training centre in a special troop train and headed north along the east coast passing through Edinburgh, across the Firth of Forth railway bridge and then on to our destination at St. Andrews. The world famous golfing town.

After disembarking we marched across the golf course and set up camp a few fields away from the golf course. We were to be under canvas and our tents were round in shape with seven or eight in a tent. The camp covered two or three grass fields, part of which was wooded and I remember that the cookhouse was in this area. The fact that the battalion was under canvas created a problem with regard to the outside cookhouse. This was situated in the wooded area of the camp and we found that the cookhouse always attracted rats and mice. The chief culprits were the rats. They would build their burrows around or near the cookhouse and that one of our tasks, at frequent intervals was to try and keep the number of rats down. It was of course very important that from a hygiene point of view, and also as far as the health of the battalion was concerned, the problem should be tackled.

Our first objective was to locate the burrows which were often concealed in the undergrowth by weeds and long grass. We would trace the burrows or rat holes and then, armed with jugs of boiling hot water supplied by the cookhouse, pour it down the holes and stand by with sticks and clubs ready to kill the rats when they ran out of their holes to avoid the hot water. One had to be very quick and alert to catch the wily rats. However the system worked very well and I remember that we had to use quite a lot of hot water. The system worked for so long but it was an exercise which had to be repeated at regular intervals and it did reduce the number of rats in the area, although you could not wipe the rats out altogether.

It was Autumn when we arrived at the camp and that the only washing facility was an outside cold tap in one of the fields next to the tents and so as the days went by and the weather became colder it was very cold having to wash outside at six o'clock in the morning. Because of the water situation the battalion used to organise special visits to the St. Andrews public baths once a week when we could enjoy a good hot shower.

Life under canvas created a few hygiene problems with our blankets which were not properly cleaned often enough and some suffered from impetigo caused by dust and dirt accumulating in the blankets. Because of this it was necessary for us to have all our clothes fumigated in St. Andrews at regular intervals.

This was one of the hazards of life under canvas with the tents being relatively small and only accommodating about eight colleagues. Our job at St. Andrews was to patrol the sand dunes and beaches along the coast line within a certain distance of the town. The town itself is a well known university town as well as being the headquarters of British golf. There are some very fine buildings in the town and the members of our battalion seemed to get on quite well with the people of St. Andrews.

The invasion scare was still in being and this was the reason for tightening up the defences in the coastal areas of this country in order to make sure that there was no easy access available to the enemy in the less populated areas of the coast line. Most of our time was taken up with patrols combined with route marches along the coastal routes.

Depression was a major problem in the forces during the war and all sections of the forces were affected. Even in our battalion a major took his life by jumping in front of an oncoming train at our local railway station. Personnel would be granted leave and did not return to their units. This was one of the jobs which fell to the military police. In addition to the regular job of "Policing" the "Redcaps" had to trace the offenders and bring them back to their army units. After four or five months under canvas we were very pleased to be given the good news that we were to return to our infantry training base. And so the battalion was on the move once again, this time the venue was to be our familiar "brick" establishment known as Queen Elizabeth Barracks, Strensall, near York.

Chapter 9.

Holt, Norfolk.
January 1943 to December 1943.

My final move before transferring to the Royal Navy took place in January 1943 my destination was to be Gresham Schools which was situated about one mile from the small village of Holt. I remember that it was a cold winter and that snow was on the ground at the time of arrival. The billet was one of the best that I had enjoyed so far in the Army. Gresham Schools was a public school before the war. The buildings were of brick and consisted of officer's quarters, kitchen, recreation rooms and of course a separate building for other ranks. The other ranks' building, I remember was part of the school's sleeping quarters. The school stood in spacious grounds consisting of grounds and gardens, a playing field which was used for recreational purposes with football in the winter months and a sports field in the summer. The sports field was also used for brigade athletics meetings. Our physical training instructor was Albert Geldard, a professional footballer who, before the war, played for Everton and England, he was an outside right.

Apart from the infantry training centre at Queen Elizabeth Barracks at Strensall, this was the only time that the battalion had a physical training instructor. The instructors at Strensall were mainly former boxers, because the commanding officer was keen on boxing and the centre arranged boxing matches between the new recruits. It was at Holt that I was able to use my clerical ability in the signal platoon. The signal sergeant had an office and I was given the job of looking after the clerical work involved in the signal platoon. I was given this job about two months before I left the army and transferred as a volunteer to the Royal Navy.

Before then our job was on coastal patrols, lots of route marches covering the coast going from village to village. In our free time we usually visited the village pubs of Holt, or made a short train journey to the seaside resorts of Sheringham or Cromer, which are only between four or six miles away from the camp. Also if the weather was fine we used to walk to the coastal town of Wells on Sea which

My brother Frank, who served in the R.A.F. and
myself taken at home whilst on leave in 1941.

was about five miles north of Holt. I remember it was very dark at
night there being no lights of course because of the enforced
"Blackout" and you had to keep strictly to the roads otherwise you
could easily get lost. During the winter months our recreation was
football and our physical training instructor used to organise knockout
competitions with seven-a-side teams and savings certificates were

given to the winners and runners up to encourage us to take part in sport. We always looked forward to these tournaments.

In the summer the battalion organised various distance races and I remember taking part in a three mile race, soon after the race had got under way a thunderstorm broke out and everywhere was flooded including the playing field, but we enjoyed the exercise essential in the army.

One of the highlights of that summer was a visit of Her Majesty the Queen (now the Queen Mother) in July. She was the Colonel in Chief of the K.O.Y.L.I. I was looking forward to seeing Her Majesty, but unfortunately on the same day our battalion relay team (which I was a member) was due to travel to London to take part in an inter-services relay team competition. It was a 12 mile relay race with a team of four runners each running three miles. I was fortunate to be selected for this team for it meant a week-end in the capital all expenses paid.

The entry consisted of about forty different teams from all the services including army, navy, airforce and civil defence. The race was to take place at the White City Stadium. So the team, plus a couple of officers set off for White City by train on the Friday afternoon. The team stayed at a big hotel on The Embankment and the race took place on the Saturday afternoon. I ran the last leg and the team did very well finishing 22nd out of the 40 teams. There were a number of famous runners taking part including the English international Sidney Wooderson, who was running in the Army Pay Corps team. The relay team race started in the White City Stadium and because each leg was 3 miles long it was necessary to complete the distance out of the stadium on the surrounding roads, returning for the last lap in the stadium. On the roads outside the stadium I remember men on cycles were encouraging the runners on their way round the course. I might add that our best runner in the team was Bandsman Jack Watson, who came from York. He was a member of the regimental band and was one of a number of people with whom I corresponded with after the war. He was also one of two army personnel whom I actually met after the war. The team stayed in

London Saturday and Sunday returning to Holt on Sunday evening. We were a training battalion at Holt and many recruits volunteered for service abroad. One of my colleagues who joined up at the same time as me at Strensall in 1940, Private Hamblett, was one of those who volunteered to go abroad and joined a K.O.Y.L.I. battalion in Italy. Unfortunately he stood on a mine and lost both his legs. I was given this information when I met a member of his battalion in Naples after I was transferred to the Royal Navy in December 1943.

During our patrol work on the east coast we did a special guard of the coastal town of Gorlston for a period of between two or three weeks. Our signal officer at this time was a young man, a "Cockney", Lieut. Galley, he saw service later in Italy. Whilst at the depot in Holt he used to say to me, "Oh, you come from Hull don't you. Top side t'Humber." At least he knew his geography.

He got on well with his men and was well liked. Towards the end of the Summer of 1943 an order came from the Admiralty asking for volunteers from our signal platoon to transfer to the Royal Navy as signalmen. The only snag was that the successful applicants, including myself, had to pass a very severe eyesight test. Everyone serving in the forces used to say, "never volunteer for anything". However, when the chance came for me to transfer to the Royal Navy, after a great deal of thought, I made the decision to volunteer.

About 30 signalmen applied, but only about half passed the eyesight test. I did not know at the time but the War Lords at the Admiralty were worried because we were losing too many warships, mainly by U-boat attack, and their trained personnel. It was therefore decided to transfer a number of trained army signalmen to the Royal Navy and in so doing reduce the amount of time spent in training specialist communications ratings. The idea behind the thinking was that to train new personnel from "Civvy Street" would take a great deal longer.

The eyesight tests were split up into two sections involving two separate visits to eye specialists in the town of Norwich. I remember that the first visit was to see if you were colour blind, fortunately I came through "with flying colours!"

My sister Doreen, who served in the A.T.S. and I
taken at home whilst on leave in 1942.

Taken whilst on leave from Holt, Norfolk in 1943.

Then came the crucial test, which was a test of one's general eyesight, this proved to be quite an extensive test which took a good deal longer than the "colour blindness" tests. After taking the tests we had to wait a few weeks before we knew who had passed, fortunately I was one of the lucky ones and my eyesight was proven to be A1. Those taking part in the eyesight tests enjoyed two days away from the camp at Holt which wasn't bad.

Now there were no barriers to prevent me from becoming a signalman in the Royal Navy. We were informed that we would be transferred from the army to the Royal Navy in December 1943. I felt sorry for the dozen or so who had applied for a transfer from our battalion and had failed the eyesight tests. They would of course remain with the battalion. We were also informed that once we were in the Royal Navy we would have to attend signal courses to learn the different procedures carried out in the senior service.

After nearly four years in the army I realised that although the change from one service to another was a big one to make, and that it was not going to be an easy ride in the Royal Navy; I knew, for example, from friends and relations that the food was better in the Royal Navy than in the Army, but on the other hand no matter which service one belonged there were risks to be taken, so the idea of a change seemed at the time to be a good one.

When the time came for me to leave the army it was with mixed feelings because the training centre at Holt, as it turned out, was one of the best that I had experienced during the whole time that I had served in the army. The conditions were good and there were happy relations with the staff and colleagues; and that was rare in the army.

In addition I was one of the training staff at the time of the transfer. At most camps there was always a bad tempered sergeant or sergeant major. However, I had made my decision to take advantage of the transfer which was on offer.

Chapter 10.

Bits and Pieces

Religion.

This chapter is devoted to odd items which occurred in my army career which were difficult to remember and also to place within the correct year. The first item concerns religion. When one was conscripted or volunteered into the forces, one had to declare one's religion; Church of England, Methodist, Catholic, etc. Whilst at my original base at the Queen Elizabeth Barracks at Strensall, we were fortunate that we had the village church of Strensall (Church of England) at our disposal. Whilst in training we had church parades once a month, when we used to march to church from the barracks accompanied by the K.O.Y.L.I. regimental band which also played in the church.

On other occasions whilst at different camps throughout the United Kingdom I used to attend various church services of different denominations. Whilst stationed in Scotland I personally found the Church of Scotland service quite different from the English church service. Over the period of time whilst serving in the army I met various colleagues who were very religious and every evening before turning into bed for the night would kneel down and say their prayers. I certainly admired them for their courage and their belief.

In the wrong "Outfit".

During the War you had to train with all sorts of different types of men and women, some you got on better with than others, but whilst in the forces one had to work together and so one had to make the best of the situation in whatever training you had to undertake.

We had one young lad in our platoon at Strensall who really wanted to be a pilot in the Royal Air Force, and at Strensall there were quite a number of aerodromes within the vicinity of the training camp. When the bombing of Germany began we used to get planes flying over the camp towards the North Sea and then on to the Continent. Every time the planes came over at night he would listen for them, and then he would go to the barrack room windows and cheer them on their way. This was of course night flying and also he knew exactly what kind of bombers they were up above. Whether he eventually made it to the R.A.F. or not, I never knew.

Telephone Operator.

Whilst in the Gloucestershire area, the battalion had a request for help at the battalion headquarters communications room. They required a relief telephone operator for one week to deputise whilst one of their operators went on leave; I got the job. It was a question of operating the switch board which included several lines. These involved the commanding officer, the adjutant and other senior officers. We had a sergeant in charge of the office. In order to operate the system successfully one had to get used to using the switchboard properly, and to make sure that you did not get your lines crossed. Once again it was something different from the ordinary army routine. It was a sitting down job too!

Ordnance Depot - Interviews.

Another exercise which the army undertook was to interview army personnel from our battalion when we were stationed near Winchester. The idea was to find out if recruits had any hidden talent which the army might use to their advantage; i.e. if recruits had knowledge of foreign languages or other technical knowledge. What we had to do was to line up one by one and we would be interviewed, asking various questions as to abilities etc. In my particular case I had a little knowledge of accountancy but unfortunately I had only just started my studies when war broke out, so that my accountancy training was limited. So that was the end of another interesting day!

Freedom of the City of York

During the early part of the year 1941 when I had returned to Strensall from hospital in Scotland for further training, the Kings Own Yorkshire Light Infantry training centre was honoured by being given the Freedom of the City of York. This meant that a number of trainees were selected to march through the streets of York with rifles and bayonets fixed, marching behind the regimental band. I was one of the lucky ones and it turned out to be a day to be remembered.

Part 2. In the Royal Navy

Chapter 11.

Seamanship Training.

I left Holt, an army infantry training centre, together with about a dozen or so army colleagues on the 9th December 1943 arriving at H.M.S. Royal Arthur (ex Butlin's Camp Skegness) later in the day.

Soon after arrival, we exchanged our army uniform for the naval uniform, quite a novelty, although we had one member of the group who had served in all three services starting off as a pilot in the R.A.F. he was grounded and then eventually transferred to the army and thence to the Royal Navy. Soon after our arrival at the new camp we contacted some of the naval personnel who were already there and we told them that we had been transferred from the army to the navy. Their first reaction was to say, quote, "You must be crazy to join this outfit." However later experiences indicated that we had definitely made the right move. So began ten days seamanship training which included learning all about ropes and the various knots used in the navy, how to sling a hammock, the various naval terms, the watch keeping times, naval language, etc. We also had instructions on rowing a boat, which took place in Butlin's boating lake! Also lifeboat drill etc., with life belts.

It was difficult at first learning how to adapt to the life as a sailor after serving nearly four years as a soldier. However the living conditions were very good whilst training and the Butlin's camp had first class conditions, including a very modern cinema where we sat in comfort and watched films after training. There was also a very good canteen with plenty of good food. At this period of the war the food in the navy was of a higher standard than that which we had in the army.

Back to training, we also learnt about the different parts of a warship, the different decks, different ranks, port and starboard, mess decks etc. We had only ten days to learn as much as possible about the working of the navy which was in my view not long enough. However we had a job to do and our main task, as far as the Royal

New Recruit
Signalman H Litchfield No. JX674294
Home port, H.M.S. Victory, Portsmouth
December 1943.

Navy was concerned, was to become an efficient signalman as soon as possible. The next step was to learn all about the signal system used by the Royal Navy, and so the next part of our training was to join the Royal Navy Signal Training School on the Isle of Man; H.M.S. Valkarie.

Chapter 12.

H.M.S. Valkarie, Isle of Man.

This was a shore based signal training centre housed in one or two of the big hotels on the sea front at Douglas Isle of Man. You literally walked out of the centre onto the beach and sea front at Douglas. In order to reach the centre we travelled by train to Liverpool on the 8th January 1944. It was mid winter and we were then transferred to the cross channel steamer to the Isle of Man. The journey in bad weather took several hours. I remember that I made a number of trips to and from the mainland during the course including seven days leave and the crossings were never very smooth.

On one particular trip equipment on the deck of the steamer had to be lashed to the deck to prevent it from rolling off the steamer, the sea was so rough. One thing that stuck in my mind was the hooting of a fog warning which used to go off regularly in misty weather since the course was during the winter months.

Our training consisted of learning the different ship manoeuvres, formations, etc., as well as learning all the different flags used in signal procedures including, also, the international flag codes which are different to the one used in the Royal Navy. We also had to learn the different types of visual signalling methods used; i.e. signalling by vision with 12 inch lamps and also the smaller aldis lamps. There was also the semaphore system of flag signalling. The various ship manoeuvres which had to be translated into flag signals was also part of our training. These manoeuvres were put into practice on the beach using marching orders and I remember spending many mornings marching up and down the beach executing these manoeuvres.

We were billeted in a hotel building close to the headquarters on the sea front, one could not wish for better accommodation. In many respects it was like going back to school again, there were various classrooms and lecture rooms which were used for signal training. We had a set programme each week with a mixture of indoor and outdoor activities. Physical training was part of the programme. We had regular P.T. sessions with instructors, in addition we did some cross country running which took place along the huge promenade which was several miles long. I remember taking part in a two mile cross country race and I finished in the first ten.

The signal course was to last sixteen weeks and we were given seven days leave in the middle of the course, a most welcome relief from training. We did get our evenings free but because it was winter time we were not able to enjoy the weather or the countryside as much as if it was summer time. However we did enjoy short trips from time to time although we could not wander about the island at will in war time, in fact we were restricted to within a few miles of Douglas. When we did get some good weather, which was not very often, the countryside around Douglas harbour was very pleasant. The next place to Douglas was Peel where there was a prisoner of war camp.

The Isle of Man was famous for three things; kippers, cats without tails, and the T.T. motor cycle races. I was able to send some kippers home and I am sure they were enjoyed by the family. Of course the T.T. motor cycle race was not run during the war. Towards the end of the course in early April the weather began to improve which enabled us to enjoy more of the countryside. At the end of the course we had to face another stormy crossing on the steamer taking us back from Douglas to the mainland and then on to H.M.S. Collingwood.

Chapter 13.

H.M.S. Collingwood, Fareham, Hampshire.

I joined this Signal Training School together with the personnel from the Isle of Man on the 19th April 1944. This was a modern training school situated at Fareham in Hampshire about fifteen miles from Southampton on the south coast. The school concentrated on reading and sending messages visually which included lamp and semaphore. At this school, Wrens worked on the administration side. The course was to last three months. One of the features of the school was a sizeable parade ground. We were accommodated in wooden huts with about twenty to a hut. In the evenings after training we were able to visit Fareham, a large village, but the favourite resort was Southampton which offered a good deal in the way of entertainment including cinemas, canteens, etc.

We were now into the better weather and there was pleasant countryside to be enjoyed. This was the beginning of the build up for the invasion of Europe known as "The Second Front" and everywhere you went, you met vehicles and troops on the move gathering for the great offensive which was to commence early in June.

Of course at that time we did not know that the offensive was to commence in the near future but we had an idea that some operation was imminent because of the build up of troops etc. One month after the "D-Day" landing on the continent the German flying bombs started coming over this country from France.

The first lot of bombs were known as V.1s or "doodlebugs", they were flying bombs powered by a jet engine and when they had reached their target area the engine would cut out, then you knew that the bomb would dive to the ground causing a great deal of destruction. It was whilst I was at Fareham that I first encountered the flying bomb.

It occurred one night after leaving the training school, I and a colleague were walking on a country road when a flying bomb appeared overhead not very far away. Luckily there was a ditch alongside the road which we jumped into for cover. Fortunately the

**H.M.S. Collingwood, Signal Training School,
Fareham, Hampshire.**
These were all ex-army personnel, I am on the back row, extreme right

bomb landed about a mile away and so we continued on our journey. Whilst we were on the signal course we had an additional task to perform in the evenings after our daily training. This was fire watching in Southampton. The city and port was one of the main targets for enemy aircraft and our job was to assist the fire fighters during night air raids. We were taken by lorry to fire watch in certain buildings in Southampton arriving about 7 p.m. and we remained on duty until the early hours of the morning. Fortunately we did not have any serious fires to deal with during our tour of duty which lasted about a month. However the extra duties on top of the training during the day made life tiring during that particular period.

My second encounter with the flying bomb took place when I had a 48 hour pass to Croydon where I spent the night in a friend's house, flying bombs were dropping around the house all night long.

Luckily the bombs missed the house but the following morning when we left, a flying bomb appeared above the roof tops of the street, we took cover under a brick wall and the bomb dropped about one hundred yards further down the street, a narrow escape.

I learnt afterwards that Croydon was one of the target areas for the flying bombs and over a period of time 142 bombs were dropped. After the completion of the signal course I returned to my base which was to be H.M.S. Victory, Portsmouth.

Having arrived there I was to await my posting for my first ship. It was now July 1944 and I did not have very long to wait at the depot. I believe it was about one week when I got a posting to the Mediterranean. I was given 7 days leave.

Chapter 14.

Malta and the Mediterranean.

The posting was to the base at Malta - H.M.S. St Angelo. Before leaving Portsmouth I was fitted out with tropical kit and I was to board a troop train for Liverpool prior to joining a convoy of troop ships bound for Naples Bay. On the train journey to Liverpool I was told that one of the naval ratings in the next carriage to us was Ivy Benson's husband. Ivy was the band leader of the all-women dance band which was well known at that time.

The convoy consisted of several ocean going liners including the "Empress of Britain", "Empress of Australia", I think there were five or six liners in all including the Dutch liner S.S. Volundam, the ship that I was to travel in convoy with the rest of the liners.

The Dutch liner was about 20,000 tons. We left Liverpool early on the 17th July 1944 in convoy and after leaving harbour we were met by an escort of destroyers out at sea. Whilst on the troop ship you could either volunteer to "work ship", i.e. to do watches or general duties, fatigues, etc. I volunteered to carry out general duties on the voyage. I can't remember how many navy personnel were on each ship but it must have been over a thousand.

The majority of the lower deck personnel slept down below in the hold of the ship which was very vulnerable in the event of a torpedo attack. Night time was the worst because of the fear of attack from German U-boats. From Liverpool we headed westwards across part of the Atlantic for a few days before heading south for Gibraltar. The sea was relatively smooth for the time of the year. The journey so far was uneventful with our escort always in position within sight of the convoy. After two days in the Atlantic we could see the Rock of Gibraltar in the distance and then we knew that we would be shortly entering the Straits of Gibraltar and then on into the Mediterranean.

It was now considerably warmer and we were looking forward to our final destination which was Naples Bay. We proceeded through the Mediterranean with Malta in the distance on our starboard side. Although my destination was Malta the convoy was to complete its voyage to Naples Bay and then I would have to make another journey to Malta. One thing I noticed on board the troopship was the quality of the drinking water which deteriorated as we proceeded on our journey. In those days fresh water had to be stored in huge tanks on board at the beginning of the journey and rationed during the journey en route.

We finally reached our destination, Naples Bay with the famous "Vesuvius Volcano" in the distance. There is a saying "see Naples and die", what a marvellous sight it was. With regard to the volcano I have since learnt that it erupted in the summer of 1944 and killed 26 people. Of course I did not know that fact at the time. Another unusual sight was to see all the troopships together in the bay. I think there were six or seven liners in the convoy. All the troopships were painted in Battleship Grey for the duration of the war. After holding my breath on seeing the marvellous sight it was time to move on. I was here for a purpose and I had to go ashore and find transport to take me to my destination which was of course Malta. In the meantime the huge liners would soon disburse to their various allotted destinations.

After landing ashore the next part of my journey to Malta was to be made aboard a local passenger ferry. The distance was about 100 miles. Naples Bay was like a mill pond when we left. I can't remember how many naval ratings were on the ferry but I would say about 30 to 40. The scenery was really beautiful. The ferry journey took about 5 hours and on approaching Valetta harbour the first impression you get is a sight of the ancient buildings on the island.

On going ashore we passed by the small caves in the rock which were used as air raid shelters during the siege of Malta in the period from 1940 to 1943. The main shore base of H.M.S. St. Angelo is on an island next to the Grand Harbour. The base was full at this particular time and so my destination was an overflow depot just next to the Grand Harbour. The accommodation consisted of a dozen big marquees or tents which were a substitute for a barrack room.

Situated around the marquees there was an office or guard room with a brick built galley where our meals were prepared. The depot also had a huge flag staff which was used for the various ceremonies

Sunny Valetta.
Malta in July 1944.

including "Sunrise and Sunset" which I took part in on several occasions. Each marquee accommodated 12 to 14 naval ratings.

It was now the middle of July and I was waiting for a posting to my first ship. It was just a question of carrying out a daily routine of fatigues during the day and enjoying the amenities offered by the Island of Malta. There was plenty to offer including some very decorative churches and other historic buildings throughout the island. The food on shore establishments in the Royal Navy was always better than the food aboard ships at sea. Weather-wise Malta was usually very sunny with average temperatures in the 80 degrees Fahrenheit range but in the winter months average temperatures were about 10 degrees lower. Like most major ports Valetta had its "red light district" which was known by sailors as the "Gut" but apart from that area the town had plenty of places of interest with some good shops in spite of the enemy bombing in the early years of the war. Valetta has a very narrow "Green Belt" and apart from this belt the soil is very sandy with rocks everywhere.

For tourists and holiday makers in peace time there are numerous beautiful churches with mosaic ceilings and they are generally very decorative. There are also some very impressive government buildings built in stone. Another attraction is the catacombs, some very old caves. The majority of people in Malta speak English but there is quite a lot of Arabic spoken. In our time, when not on duty, a favourite place was the balcony overlooking the Grand Harbour. There you could witness the "comings and goings" of the Royal Navy ships in the area. Unfortunately Malta is not now a port for ships of the Royal Navy. I remember during my stay in Malta watching several convoys, one of which included 5 aircraft carriers, a supply ship and a British cruiser, probably on its way to the eastern Mediterranean.

The conditions that existed during the war, no one except the participants, knew what was going on as far as the conduct of the war was concerned. Even if you were sent abroad you did not know your destination until you were half way there. However security was a high priority during the war and without it you could not count on success. There were slogans such as "Walls have Ears" and "Be like Dad keep Mum". Of course we did hear radios putting out news in the canteens, Y.M.C.A.s etc. and of course you could hear the news in one's home but the government of the day put out what it wanted the public to hear. The Germans did exactly the same. Whilst in Malta I heard in my letters from home that my brother Frank's best friend, a flight sergeant in the R.A.F. was shot down over Malta in 1943, and that he was buried in a military cemetery in Malta. He had completed the statutory number of bombing raids over Germany, (I think it was 40 trips), he was then given leave before leaving with a squadron for Malta.

Unfortunately my stay in Malta was not long enough for me to make the necessary enquiries as to exactly where he was buried. Whilst in Malta I had my photograph taken in tropical gear by a street trader taken amongst the palm trees which came out quite well and it is still in my possession. The weather during my stay was on the whole, dry and sunny. However one day in August we did experience a "Tropical Storm" which built up soon after tea time with high winds and dust storms.

I remember the storm broke between seven and eight o'clock with thunder, lightning and torrential rain, it was none stop for 3 or 4 hours. Several of our marquees were either blown down completely or partially blown down, and most of the marquees had two feet of water in them. Luckily our marquee was not badly damaged. However we had two feet of water to cope with and when it was all over, and the sun was shining again, our first job was to get rid of the water and tidy the marquees up to some sort of order ready for work. I was kept awake all night watching the storm, but one of the ratings in our marquee slept through the storm in his bed with water all around him. Nearly fifty years after the end of the war in Europe the Maltese Government decided to strike a war medal for service personnel who had taken part in the siege of Malta between the years 1940 and 1943. My brother in law, Edmund Carroll obtained a medal. He spent some time in the Mediterranean, including trips to Malta and although I was stationed in Malta in 1944 I did not qualify for a medal.

Chapter 15.

H.M.S. Stuart Prince.

At last after nearly two months of waiting for my posting, news came through towards the end of August. I was to join a converted merchant ship of about 10,000 tons, her name was Stuart Prince. She was at the moment in Naples Bay. She was an old merchant ship and was basically a radar training ship. She had on board a number of radar sets and other instruments and these were used to train naval ratings in the art of detection and the use of radar.

Of course radar at the time was something new and was only developed during the war years. The ship also had a huge revolving aerial fixed on the upper deck which was about twenty feet across. The ship's top speed was only about 10 knots (13 miles per hour) and she was coal fired. In order to join the Stuart Prince I had to travel as a passenger aboard the cruiser H.M.S. Sirius which took me from Valetta to Naples Bay. During the journey, the cruiser carried out gunnery practice with her ten inch guns. It was a new experience for me and one that I shall always remember. During the practice which lasted for about half an hour the noise from the guns was nerve racking. However after about two hours the ship arrived in Naples Bay and I was put on one of the cruiser's barges and we headed for the Stuart Prince which was at anchor not far from Naples.

This was my first ship and I climbed up the rope ladder with my kit bag and landed on the deck. I then saluted the quarter deck and so began my stay on Stuart Prince. The signal staff consisted of a petty officer yeoman of signals and five signalmen. The captain of the ship had the rank of commander and was one of the old school.

He was very keen to show his authority and was not very well liked. The same could be said of the yeoman but we had to work with them, and work as a team on board ship. This was the difference I found between being in the army and being in the navy. In the army if you made a mistake only yourself suffered whereas in the navy if you made an error of judgement or a mistake, the rest of the ship's company could suffer. I learnt later that the ship took part in the allied landings in the south of France at Marseilles before I joined the ship, although I never found out exactly what the ship's roll was.

For the next three months we were to remain in the Mediterranean taking part in various exercises in the bay with the other ships. I remember that there were two cruisers, an aircraft carrier and a destroyer in the area at the time, but the numbers altered from time to time. The signal exercises which I was involved in were controlled by the senior ship which was in the bay at the time of the exercise. These exercises were visual signals which involved flag signals only. The controller (the senior ship) would send a message to all the naval ships taking part in the exercises in the bay and the yeoman of signals would read the message with his binoculars and then give us (the signalmen) the reply. We had to translate the reply with the appropriate flags. The object of the exercises was to hoist the flags as quickly as possible on to the ship's halyards, and the ship with the quickest reply obtained a point. The messages kept on coming and the exercises usually lasted on average about two hours each day. Of course we had difficulty in competing against the bigger capital ships because they could call upon more staff to take part in the exercises.

However it was a job that we had to carry out and we also had to contend with the yeoman of signals "letting off steam" from time to time but we had to take part. A pleasant relief at this time was the fact that we were allowed shore leave, subject to watch keeping and a visit to Naples was always interesting.

At this particular time the allies had taken Rome about four weeks before I joined the ship so the Germans were not so far away. Naples was a town which was ravaged by war by the Germans and venereal disease was common amongst the female population. During one of my trips ashore at Naples I met one of my colleagues from my army days; Private Silverman of the Kings Own Yorkshire Light Infantry, he was based in Italy. He was a table tennis player and so we headed for one of the table tennis centres in Naples, but unfortunately all the tables were fully booked for some time and so we were unable to have a game. In any case I was only ashore for four hours. He told me that my old Signal Officer Lt. Galley, formally at Holt, Norfolk, was now with them and that a colleague who had joined the army at the same time as myself, Private Hamblett had unfortunately trodden on a mine in Italy and had lost both his legs; a great tragedy for such a young man. However we had a good chat and I was very pleased to see him. Early in November 1944 the ship received orders to proceed back to the United Kingdom. When these orders came through to the ship I wondered, in view of the fact that I had only been in the Mediterranean for five months I might have been given orders to go back to my depot at H.M.S. St. Angelo at Malta. However the good news was that I remained with Stuart Prince and I would return home with the ship.

Of course I was very pleased to hear the news. Our destination was to be the Firth of Clyde not far from Glasgow. We were to proceed from Naples Bay back home to the United Kingdom on our own. The ship had very little protection if we were attacked, but we did have some Ack-Ack guns in case of air attacks. Another disadvantage was that our maximum speed was only about 12 knots.

It was the first week in November that we left the Bay of Naples and our first port of call was to be Gibraltar. Since this was my first ship, watches at sea were new to me, however there was always more than one signalman on watch at the same time so that I soon got into the routine of receiving and sending messages.

On arriving at Gibraltar we had to "coal ship", this meant all hands on deck except communications ratings, petty officers and of course officers, so we were able to go ashore whilst the operation was in progress. Coaling ship involved a great deal of hard work with shovels and many hands (sailors). It was also a very dirty job and looking down on the operation from the bridge reminded me of the "Black and White Minstrels". Of course the modern ships now have diesel engines, not the old fashioned coal burning engines. It certainly was an unusual sight to witness. I did manage to go ashore at this particular time and I, together with another signalman and a leading seaman, passed a naval officer a short distance away so we did not bother to salute him. However the officer called over to us to stop and gave us a lecture because we had failed to salute him. He asked what ship we were from and when we told him our ship's name he said that our captain would be hearing from him.

The leading seaman who was with us was worried in case he would be reduced to the rank of seaman. Luckily nothing further was heard from the officer and so that was the end of the matter. We only stayed at Gibraltar for the time necessary to coal the ship. Whilst ashore my signalman colleague and I paid a visit to the Y.M.C.A. where they were giving a concert, but to our dismay the main item on the programme was an act by Spanish women dancing with castanets, they danced very well but after a while the dancing became a bit boring, we much preferred to have a good laugh with a comedy artist; there is nothing like a change in the daily routine, especially in war time.

We duly left Gibraltar and set our sights on home waters. Very soon we were nearing the United Kingdom and home waters when the weather began to turn really cold, we were now into Winter at the end of November. It was not long before we entered St. George's Channel proceeding towards the Irish Sea keeping close to the west coast of Britain. We were now well on our way towards our ultimate goal, the Firth of Clyde. We finally arrived in Scottish waters on the 23rd of December 1944 and dropped anchor in Gourock. This was the anchorage for all warships, big or small. It was decided by the captain that half of the ship's company should go on Christmas leave and that the other half would have New Year leave. I believe we were only granted 3 or 4 days leave. However I was to go home for the New Year and it turned out to be the first time during the war that I had managed to get some leave at Christmas time. I spent all the Christmas days (six in all) during the war away from home. After returning from leave I remember that we were to experience a cold winter.

We had quite a lot of ice and snow on the ship's flag deck and the communications ratings had the job of removing the ice and snow with various pick axes etc. For the next three months the ship remained in Scottish waters steaming along the western coastline including a visit to the Isle of Arran and also a Degaussing exercise

off the island to neutralise the ship's magnetism in order to prevent
the ship detonating magnetic mines. On our visit to the Isle of Arran
after Degaussing we asked permission to enter the harbour at
Lamlash, permission was given by the harbour master but the boom
across the harbour was not open by the time the ship reached the
boom and consequently we had to make an emergency reversal of
the ship's engines just missing a collision with the boom. However
the boom eventually opened and we arrived safely in the harbour.
We made several patrols along the Scottish lakes and coastline and
it was winter time and consequently on a few occasions we
experienced dense fog and so we had to sound the ship's fog horn
every minute or so. It was very dangerous when visibility was very
bad. On one occasion whilst at sea, I think we were actually in the
Irish Sea when we received a report that a German U-boat was in
the vicinity. We had to race for Port at full speed which was only
about 12 knots. We did manage to escape an attack from the U-boat.
    We spent most of our time in the Gourock Waters and the Irish
Sea. The Gourock Waters was the anchorage for all the ships leaving
and returning from the Atlantic. The liners Queen Mary and Queen
Elizabeth were troopships operating from the Clyde carrying troops
to and from America. We had quite a number of capital ships in
our company as well as aircraft carriers, cruisers and destroyers.
The captain of Stuart Prince had a son, a first lieutenant serving
on one of the destroyers which escorted "The Queens" in and out
of the Clyde.
    While we were in Scottish waters he would visit his father from
time to time. The Queens did not need to be escorted across the
Atlantic because of the high speed that they travelled when making
the crossing.
    They were however given protection by the destroyers when
nearing port because of the risk of U-boats which quite often lay in
waiting to attack the Queens when they were nearing their destination
after crossing the Atlantic. Happily the German U-boats were not
successful and the Queens made many crossings carrying troops to
and from America. The way they worked was that the Queen

Elizabeth would start from the Clyde and the Queen Mary would start from New York so that both ships were never in the same place at the same time. We had a scare in the anchorage one very windy day when we had four aircraft carriers at anchor and the wind was blowing at gale force causing one of the aircraft carriers to drag her anchor. A collision was just avoided with another ship. This was in the middle of the night.

We used to get some very windy weather in the Clyde in winter time and I remember going ashore one night on leave. During the night the wind strengthened to gale force eight, which meant that I could not get back on board ship that night, so I had to spend the night in a hostel and report back to the ship the following morning.

Another point in bad weather, particularly in windy weather, steam ships had to raise steam in case of emergencies such as dragging anchors caused by high winds. The nearest loch in the Gourock Waters was Gare Loch and this particular loch was used by the Admiralty to accommodate warships which had come to the end of their useful service and they were eventually to be broken up. The loch was known as the "Warship's Grave Yard".

I remember when our ship, H.M.S. Stuart Prince got the order to proceed to Gare Loch in April 1945, quite a number of well known capital ships and cruisers were already in the loch, including the First World War battleship H.M.S. Ramilles.

The nearest village to the anchorage was Helensburgh, and we went ashore there when we moved to Gare Loch. We remained in the loch for about two weeks and then we were ordered to proceed up the Clyde to the Glasgow docks, where we were to be broken up. It was a remarkable journey along the Clyde, with ship yards on either side of the river, and warships and aircraft carriers at various stages of completion. After about a mile and a half of twists and turns in the river, we approached the Glasgow docks and were allocated a dry dock where the sea life of the converted merchant ship H.M.S. Stuart Prince came to its end. Some of the ship's company were returned to their depots straight away, but I was one of the lucky ones who stayed aboard dealing with various communication matters for about four weeks. Whilst I was in Glasgow, victory in Europe came about on the 8th May 1945, and I remember hearing the good news sitting on the ship's deck on one of the ship's radios. One week after this it was my turn to return to my depot at Portsmouth, which took place on the 17th May 1945. I was to await a further posting in my naval career.

Chapter 16.

Southampton to Hong Kong
on L.S.T. 3033 Tank Landing Ship.

I was posted from my depot at Portsmouth to the L.S.T. 3033 in June 1945. She was a brand new ship built in Sunderland and was a tank landing ship of 6500 gross tonnage with a length of 346 Feet.

She was the most modern tank landing ship built in the Second World War. She had upper and lower decks capable of carrying troops and equipment including heavy army vehicles and the ship had opening bow doors. The ship could be beached and her armourment consisted of twin Bofors "3" guns mounted forward which could be used both for Ack-Ack purposes and also for bombardment.

The Ship was what is known as "flat bottomed" and rolled badly in heavy seas. Whilst at Sunderland I was fortunate enough to take part in the commissioning ceremony and that my part as a signalman was to hoist the first White Ensign on this new ship. After commissioning the ship proceeded to Southampton via the North Sea, where we were due to join two other L.S.T.s. However one was damaged and had to go into dock for repairs and the other one broke down on its way to join us. The consequence was that we were ordered to proceed on our journey alone.

The captain usually informs the crew of the ships destination some time into the journey. We knew that we were bound for the Far East because we took tropical kit with us. I found out later that our destination was to be Hong Kong, and that we were carrying amongst other things new radio equipment to be used in a new radio station in Hong Kong. We left Southampton on the 31st July 1945 and made a short journey across Southampton Waters to Ryde in the Isle of Wight for an overnight stay before proceeding on our journey to the Far East. This was to be our last run ashore in the United Kingdom for at least six months.

Our first port of call was to be Gibraltar but before reaching the famous rock port we had to proceed through the Bay of Biscay which can be very rough at times. However the crossing this time was reasonably smooth. We had an uneventful journey reaching Gibraltar

Tiger Hunting
Photographer's Studio, Calcutta, November 1945.
I am second on the left.

H.M.S. L.S.T. 3033
Beached in Bombay harbour, September 1945.

after three or four days sailing. Our stay here was only four hours and we left Gibraltar and entered the Mediterranean. With regard to Gibraltar there is a saying that whilst the apes remain on the rock, Gibraltar will remain British. We proceeded towards our next objective which was Port Said and on our way we observed the island of Malta (now known as the George Cross Island because of the people's heroic stand and courage against the German and Italian air raids against it) which we saw in the distance on the 11th August 1945. This was the second time that I had seen Malta whilst in the navy, the first being when I was posted to the naval base in Malta H.M.S. St. Angelo. At this point the ship was ahead of its schedule and so the captain decided that we should enter a small creek near Benghazi. So we duly dropped anchor about a mile from this lonely stretch of coastline. We were able to spend four hours here and the crew had the choice of either going ashore in one of the ship's boats or staying and having a swim in the warm Mediterranean sea.

I decided to go ashore and inspect some German built concrete landing stages meant to be used as miniature harbours for landing craft. They must have been used during the desert war of 1943. Our four hours soon passed and we were underway once again. We passed Alexandria on the 14th August and arrived at Port Said early in the morning of the 15th August.

We were allowed to go ashore the following day, incidentally the captain of our ship was born in Alexandria. We arrived at Taufiq in the Suez Canal and dropped anchor in the evening of the 18th August 1945. It was whilst we were at anchor in the Suez that we heard on the radio that Japan was due to surrender at any time. As a result of this message all the ships in the vicinity decided to blow their hooters or fog signals which went on for quite a while and I was told that the officers on board had a little celebration before turning in that night.

We set sail the following day and proceeded to the Red Sea where we experienced very high temperatures. It really was very hot and we wore as little as possible during the day because of the heat.

We arrived at Aden on Friday the 24th of August and I personally had to go ashore to collect some important signal messages from the

Our L.S.T. 3033. Fully loaded in the
Indian Ocean in October 1945.

signal headquarters. We left Aden on the following day and ran into heavy seas which lasted for three days.

It was during this period whilst on signal duty that I caught sight of a shark in the distance. We were now seeing quite a number of "Flying Fish" which used to leap out of the water rather like a salmon. Many of these fish used to reach the lower decks of the ship. We were now in the Indian Ocean and proceeding in the direction of Bombay which we reached on the 1st of September. According to the ship's log we had now covered 7000 nautical miles since leaving Southampton on the 31st July last. We moved into Bombay Bay and dropped anchor. We spent seven days in the bay and I was able to go ashore and take a look at the city of Bombay. This was my first visit to India and it was a very exciting experience. I found out that most

Indians used to chew a sort of red root (called Betel Juice) which
they would spit out on to the streets.

The most impressive sight one sees in the main streets are lots of
cows and oxen roaming about going just where it takes their fancy.
There is no control over them because they are "Sacred" therefore
they are allowed to go just where they please. Another impression
one gets is the high population of the Indian towns, of course today
their numbers must have increased considerably fifty years on. Whilst
in Bombay I managed to find a few bits and pieces in the shops
which enabled me to send a small parcel home.

We left Bombay on the 10th September and immediately ran into
rough weather. Our next destination was Colombo in Ceylon (now
known as Sri-Lanka) which we reached on the 14th September 1945.
On arrival we loaded up with troops mainly Gurkas, vehicles, trucks
etc., which were to be delivered at Singapore our next port of call.
There was a delay in leaving Colombo harbour for several hours.
Our sick bay attendant was taken to hospital ashore at Colombo and
we were promised a replacement for him. However he did not arrive
and so the captain decided to leave harbour without a sick bay
attendant; although we did get a replacement some time later. We
entered the Malaccan Straits which were famous for their marvellous
sunsets at night (brilliant red), you do not see anything like it in this
country. We saw some of the islands which were formally held by
the Japanese with various gun positions still intact.

It was not long before we entered a minefield area so we needed
escort vessels because of the mines laid by the Japanese. However
we arrived safely at Singapore. At this point in our journey from the
United Kingdom we had completed 10,000 nautical miles. Our first
task was to unload our troops and vehicles etc., and in order to do
this we had to move from our anchorage and come alongside in the
harbour.

The docks in the harbour were very heavily bombed by the
Japanese and as a result no buildings were left standing. The damage
was extensive. In spite of all the damage in the docks area Singapore
itself was not badly damaged. When we went ashore we were

On the Bridge of L.S.T. 3033
Manning the 12 inch visual signal lamp in the Indian Ocean.

Ashore in Hong Kong October 1945.

surprised to see so many activities going on, in other words the recovery by the people of Singapore was remarkable so soon after the end of the war with the Japanese Hostilities having only ceased on the 14th August 1945. We found that there was plenty to see in the shops and there were places of entertainment including a centre known as "The New World". One member of the crew managed to get a film for his camera and took a number of photographs and later I was able to obtain copies of them.

We left Singapore on the 24th September heading for Hong Kong. The seas were still heavy as we made our approach to Hong Kong. It was necessary for us to pass through channels specially swept by mine sweepers which were only three cables wide. The waters were dangerous because the whole area was mined by the enemy and only small channels had been swept by mine sweepers. The following day, on our approach to the island we had a very heavy rainstorm and bathing on the upper deck was piped. It was not long before we could see the huge Chinese mountains which appeared to come out of the water but of course they were on the Mainland. It was a spectacular scene and a moment which has always remained in my memory years after the war.

Before entering the approaches to Hong Kong we had to have an escort to guide us to the harbour because of the mines. This was arranged and we arrived safely in the harbour on the 29th September 1945. The ships log indicated that we had completed 12,200 miles so far.

When you move from one part of the world to another, you have to adjust your clocks. On arrival at Hong Kong we had to move our clocks on one hour. We were now eight and a half hours in advance of British time. On the following day we encountered very high winds and we were informed that a typhoon was on its way to our area. The result was that all capital ships in the harbour (battleships and cruisers) were ordered out to sea to ride out the storm. We of course stayed in the harbour. Fortunately the typhoon had changed direction and we only got the edge of the storm although a number of small ships and "Sampans" were sunk. It turned out that the capital ships

H.M.S. L.S.T. 3033 beached on Stonecutters Island,
Hong Kong harbour, 5th October 1945.

On the deck of H.M.S. L.S.T. 3033, beached on
Stonecutters Island, Hong Kong.
From left to right; Petty Officer Thompson, Able Seaman Holder and myself.

Hong Kong Harbour, November 1945.
In the foreground is our L.S.T. 3033 and in the background is
Aircraft Carrier H.M.S. Pioneer

had in fact moved further towards the storm and had come off worse. We originally beached in the Taikoo Docks but then returned to our anchorage in the bay near to Stonecutters Island.

We stayed at our anchorage for a further two days during which time the sun was very hot and most of the ratings were affected by the heat. On the 5th of October we moved from the bay and beached on Stonecutters Island, a small island in the harbour. We beached on the island in the early morning and so the first thing we did was to explore the island which was not very big, in fact it was about half a mile square and was covered with trees, shrubs and green grass; it was hilly in parts. I understand that it is now a nature reserve full of various birds and animals. The island has also been featured in a B.B.C. nature programme.

Our first run ashore in Hong Kong was on Friday 5th October 1945 and I was very surprised to see how crowded the island was. We had now completed 12,400 nautical miles in journey and after a stay of just two weeks we were ordered to proceed to Singapore. The previous day was Chinese Victory Day. Masthead flags were flown and there was a Royal salute of 21 guns by all H.M. Ships in the harbour. Later, there was also a big parade in Hong Kong and a firework display.

Chapter 17.

Singapore, our New Base.

We duly left Hong Kong on Monday the 8th October 1945 in stormy conditions with very heavy seas. Clocks were put back a further half hour. It was still a very heavy swell. We were at sea for three days with improving weather conditions. We were now seven and a half hours ahead of G.M.T. We had heavy rain in the evening of the 14th October. The following day was very calm and still no land or ships were in sight since leaving Hong Kong. Our expected day of arrival at Singapore was Wednesday 17th October and we found out that we were ahead of schedule and so the captain slowed the ship down and a revolver competition between the officers was arranged on the upper deck. Shortly after this competition we were approaching a very small rock with a cave entrance inhabited by birds and the captain took the opportunity to test the accuracy of the twin Borfar guns; the gunners duly aimed for the cave. The range was about one hundred yards. There were a number of birds which paid the price of the operation but the captain was very pleased with the accuracy of the shooting.

We duly arrived at Singapore at 10 am on the 17th October amid brilliant sunshine and, after dropping anchor, we were greeted by a number of "Over the side traders". These were the local people in small boats who would come alongside the ship in the hope of buying, amongst other things, cigarettes which were very much in demand. Non-smokers would buy some cigarettes from the ship's canteen and sell them over the side (if they were lucky enough to find a buyer). Lines were dropped into the boats and the goods would be dropped into the boat; the boat owners would then tie the currency (Malayan dollars) to the lines and this was then hauled up to our ship. This was, of course, illegal but a lot of this sort of thing went on unofficially.

The mileage from base was now 13,600. We received quite a big batch of mail and I was one of the lucky ones who received some mail from home. The following day I went ashore with two of my ship mates and managed to find a cinema. The films we saw were "Tall in the Saddle" and "Seventh Column". There was also plenty

L.S.T. 3033 at Port Dickson, Malaya.
Some of our crew in the foreground.

Unloading from our L.S.T. 3033 at Port Dickson, Malaya.
There was a number of L.S.T.s in this group which travelled in convoy.

of cafes in Singapore with a good variety of food (steak, chips and eggs, etc.). I also went ashore the following day to do a little shopping and also managed to see an E.N.S.A. concert which was very good indeed and a real morale booster. It was during this stay that the ship's doctor had a mental breakdown and another doctor from one of the ships in the harbour came along to see him; as a result he was taken ashore and into hospital.

There was quite a number of war ships in the harbour on this occasion including the cruiser "Jamaica" which was on its way home to the United Kingdom. On the following day at 0700 hours we left Singapore and arrived at Port Dickson at 9 o'clock in the evening. We dropped anchor and found the place very desolate. The following morning we were beached and were joined by two other L.S.T.s; No. 237 and No. 347. This was the first time that we were able to play football on the beach because the ship was beached. Quite a number of the crew enjoyed the exercise.

This was one of many occasions when we witnessed the glorious Malaccan sunsets with a really deep red sky. It really is a marvellous sight. Later on in the day we were to take on troops and equipment and were to sail in company with the other two L.S.Ts. We were destined for South East Asia the old capital of Batavia. En-route we saw an American battleship in the distance but we made no contact with her. We managed to acquire a young puppy from Port Dickson but I can't remember what happened to the puppy; however, in the majority of cases cats and dogs could not adapt to living aboard ship.

During the night we developed engine trouble for the first time and had to reduce speed, but after a short while the trouble was rectified and we were able to catch up with the other two L.S.T.s.

On the 25th of October we had heavy rainstorms and were still in convoy with the other two ships. This was the day that we crossed the Equator (the actual time was 06.15 a.m.) and in peace time when this happens the navy has a "Crossing the Line Ceremony" when the captain dresses up as "Old Father Time" but of course this does not happen in times of war. We had rain the following day and L.S.T.

237 parted company on her way to a different port of call. On the 27th October we had a lovely sunny day and arrived at Batavia in the Dutch East Indies; this time beached to join another four L.S.T.s, No.s; 538, 164, 347 and 248; making five in all. We found the air here very humid with very high temperatures. We were granted shore leave only until 1730 hours, which was 5.30 p.m., because we had to prepare to leave Batavia the following day together with L.S.T. 347. We were to return to Singapore which was two days sailing from Batavia.

The following day the captain decided to hold a revolver competition shooting at tiles on the deck. I took part and represented No.7 mess. It turned out to be a fine day with a lovely sunset which was typical of the Malaccan Straits.

We had now completed 16,000 nautical miles since leaving our base in the United Kingdom. The next day I was on the morning watch. The day started with a storm and we encountered the French battleship "Richelieu" also the cruiser "Clone". We arrived in Singapore at 10 a.m. and dropped anchor. The date was the 31st October 1945. I went ashore and had an enjoyable time. Our stay this time was for only two days. We received orders to proceed with L.S.T. 3504 to Calcutta.

After a further day we left with L.S.T. 3504; however, after a few hours she parted company as her destination was Rangoon. On Sunday the 4th of November we had a change in our eating arrangements. We were to change to "Canteen Messing" which simply meant that we had to get our food direct from the canteen. Every day we had an orderly on each mess who was responsible for collecting meals for that particular day. Soon after midnight we had a very heavy thunderstorm. Monday was another lovely day after the thunderstorm and I had the forenoon watch. One of my jobs that morning was to repair one of the signal halyards. Later in the day we received a signal ordering the ship to make a diversion to a small island off the Burmese coast.

Our destination was to be Kyauk Pyu-Ramree island. We had rifle firing practice on board in which I took part and I managed to get within the one-inch group of the targets, good shooting! We duly arrived at Kyauk Pyu the following day just before dark and dropped anchor in the harbour. Then followed some warm and sunny weather and being in such a remote harbour we did not keep any visual signal watches. The captain went ashore but there was no shore leave for the rest of the crew at present. We acquired a black and white cat from ashore. We painted the flag deck. Our next move was to beach on the shore soon after midday. After beaching we were allowed ashore and to visit the island which had an aerodrome. Some of the shore leave party were able to talk to the airmen and our leading signalman took some photographs of our crew. After tea we enjoyed a rare piece of recreation which we did not get a chance to participate in very often. Yes you have guessed; it was a rare game of football on the beaches which were very smooth and flat; ideal for football.

As the day drew to a close a bonus was a very spectacular evening sunset. Later that night we loaded our L.S.T. with Indian troops and military vehicles destined for Calcutta. The next day we made an attempt to leave at twelve noon, but the tide was not right so we had to wait a further twelve hours until midnight. This time we were successful but after being underway for several hours in the early morning we had trouble with the ship's bow doors, they would not close properly after loading the ship; as a result we had to stop the ship at 8.45 a.m. for one hour to rectify the fault. This was duly achieved and all was well once more.

After several more hours we were now arriving at the approaches to Calcutta so we dropped anchor to await a pilot to guide us up the river. We had to wait several hours for the pilot and on his arrival we duly weighed anchor. Whilst waiting for the pilot we had a good view of rural India with the scenery and the farm animals etc.

With the pilot safely aboard we proceeded up the river to Calcutta docks which we reached at 4 p.m. on the 15th November 1945. It was known as Kidderpore Dock. I stayed on board the following day and received the good news that a "Draft Chit" was on board for my return home and eventual discharge from the services. After six years war service it was great news. My release depended on a

Aerodrome on Kyauk Pyu Island, Burma.
Two members of our crew with empty petrol
containers. The aerodrome was used to support the
14th Army in Burma.

relief being available to replace me. The following morning I was
fortunate to accompany the ship's captain in his jeep to visit the
signals headquarters of Fort William just outside Calcutta. On the
way to the headquarters the captain asked me where I came from
(my home town) and when I told him that I came from Hull, he said
he had once posted a letter for a crew member addressed to Hull. It's
a small world.

On my return to the ship I was able to go ashore and duly celebrate
(but I did not get drunk). Whilst ashore I had bought a big leather

suitcase which I managed to bring home and it lasted many years. I also had my photograph taken with other members of the crew and a stuffed tiger; together with various weapons supplied to us to make it look more realistic, i.e. spears, rifles, etc.

The photograph is still in my possession. On Sunday the 18th November 1945, which was my birthday, the ship was loaded once again with army vehicles. L.S.T. 3007 was in the harbour and one of my colleagues aboard knew some of the crew, so we paid them a visit but we could not stay very long. Part of our cargo this time was 2000 petrol tins.

The next day I had further messages to take to the signal headquarters at Fort William and I was able to a organise a lift in a naval truck. I went ashore with one of our crew and did some shopping which included the purchase of some ladies underwear for my girl friend which caused some amusement with the shop keeper trying to decide which size would be appropriate. I found out later that a great deal of underwear in India came from the United Kingdom. On the way back to the ship that night we were involved in some riots which were taking place in the city centre. Extremists in large numbers were running down the streets carrying lighted torches, going from one street to another. When we encountered "The Mob", we dashed into the next street to avoid them. The following day all shore leave was stopped because of the riots. Because of possible disturbances when going ashore we normally went in twos or threes to avoid any trouble. We now took on board Indian troops together with their vehicles and equipment and left the docks the following day to refuel further down the river. We left the fuelling jetty the following day with a pilot on board to guide us out of the river.

Whilst waiting for the river boat to collect the pilot we were able to feed the seagulls (they were everywhere). After dropping the pilot at the entrance to the river we duly proceeded to sea. During the night we passed Rangoon in the distance. The next two days were spent at sea heading for the Malaccan Straits with good sunny weather which is what you would normally expect in this part of the World.

On approaching Singapore we had to advance our clocks again

to bring them in line with the area. Just before reaching Singapore two Indian soldiers were taken ill and so we had to send a signal to arrange for them to be dealt with on arrival in Singapore. When we arrived in Singapore it was a "red letter" day for me personally for I received a discharge message along with three other members of the crew.

Friday the 30th November 1945 was the day when I said farewell to the crew of L.S.T. 3033; six months after joining the ship when she was first commissioned in Sunderland. This was really the start of my journey home and the three of us had to report to the shore base of H.M.S. Sultan ashore in Singapore to await transport home. After reporting our first visit was to the canteen. We spent the next six days in the shore base waiting for a draft home. Whilst at the base in Singapore I met up with Leading Telegraphist Stobbs who served with me on my first ship, the converted merchant ship H.M.S. Stuart Prince, the radar training ship. I was informed of the United Kingdom draft on Wednesday the 5th December and therefore I went for my last look at Singapore in the afternoon, spending the evening in the depot canteen. I found that the food was not very good in comparison with that on board L.S.T. 3033.

Chapter 18.

My Journey Home on the Battleship H.M.S. Howe.

Our United Kingdom draft mustered at the depot on Thursday 6th December 1945 and we then knew that we were to go home on the battleship H.M.S. Howe which was at anchor in Singapore harbour. We were to join her the next day, Friday the 7th December 1945.

We landed on board the battleship from a drifter at 1000 hrs and we were to leave Singapore at 1345 hrs. We duly left harbour and the ships speed was 15 knots, an economical speed. The normal complement of the battleship was about 1200, but on this occasion as we were taking navel personnel home after serving overseas; there were over 2000 officers and ratings on board. The following morning I and other signal ratings had to report to the flag deck in order to be given duties for the voyage and I was made a "Day Man" which meant that I would only do day watches, no night watches. Because there were so many signalmen on board the day watches were well spread out which meant that your turn for watch keeping came every other day. For the first two days we had some very rough weather with heavy seas breaking over the forecastle of the ship and this became an area which was banned during heavy seas.

After five days sailing we arrived at Columbo harbour. I managed to get ashore the first day and bought four pounds of the best Ceylon tea to take home. It was contained in a sealed wooden box and was very acceptable at home because of the rationing. Whilst ashore I visited the fleet canteen and the empire cinema where I saw a film called "Sensations of 1945". We were to stay in Columbo harbour for three days. The cruiser H.M.S. London was anchored in the harbour, together with the Dutch liner The "New Amsterdam" painted in her new colours.

We were informed that she was due to arrive in the United Kingdom on the 24th December next. Today I had the first dog watch. On the last day of our stay in Columbo I went ashore and visited the naval base of H.M.S. Myina which was about five miles from Columbo. I managed to get a lift in a naval lorry which was going to the base. The reason for my visit was a possible meeting with my new brother in law, Edmund Carroll, a petty officer in the navy

H.M.S. Howe.
The battleship which was to take me and 2000 others home to Portsmouth.
This picture was taken at the beginning of the war.

H.M.S. Howe.
Taken whilst serving with the Far Eastern Fleet in January 1944.

whom I knew was in this area, but I wasn't sure whether he was at the base or not. On arriving at the camp and making enquiries I was told that he had in fact been at the camp but had left the base two weeks earlier, so my luck was out. Despite this, I enjoyed the journey amongst the tropical trees and the green countryside even though I was observing from the back of a lorry. The trees were very dense in that area.

Saturday the 15th December 1945 was a very eventful day for the ship's company; the commander in chief of the East Indies Fleet, Admiral Arthur Power, joined the ship. He was on his way home to the United Kingdom. Admiral Power was one of the group of service chiefs who took part in the Japanese surrender in August 1945.

We left Columbo at 1400 hours and I was on duty on the flag deck. This particular day I was also "Cook of the Mess" which meant that I had to collect the meals from the galley (the cookhouse). On the following day Sunday we had a religious service on board but I did not take part because I had the forenoon watch. After two days of sailing we arrived at Bombay, it was a lovely sunny day and the ship moored in midstream. The next day I did not have a watch and so I was able to attend an ENSA concert on board in the afternoon which was very good entertainment. On the 19th December I attended for the first time the ship's cinema and saw a film called "A Man Named Sullivan". What it was all about I do not recall.

We left Bombay at 9 p.m. and I was on the bridge. It was now beginning to get warmer so I decided to do some washing. On Friday the 21st December we passed the cruiser "Cumberland" and exchanged Christmas greetings. The sea was now getting rough and as a result quite a lot of spray was created. The following day I had the first dog watch. We were now heading for the Suez Canal and we were two days sailing away from the Port of Aden which we reached on Christmas Eve day at eight o'clock in the morning. It was a lovely day. On arrival we tied up to a buoy. I went ashore in the afternoon and had a good trip round Aden which is a typical Arab town. I did not have a watch this day which enabled me to go ashore.

The following day was Christmas Day, which was a very memorable day for me. It was my first and last Christmas aboard a large Royal Navy capital ship. I spent three Christmas's in the Royal Navy but only one aboard ship at sea. I spent Christmas morning on the flag deck. Captain's and admiral's Christmas rounds meant that they went round the mess decks wishing everyone "A Happy Christmas". In addition, according to tradition, officers served and distributed each mess with Christmas dinners on the lower decks. We all enjoyed our Christmas dinner consisting of turkey and Christmas pudding. Pipe down was at nine thirty in the morning, meaning that there would be no work after this time apart from duty watches. I took part in the Christmas day "Sunset" (1641 hours), the lowering of the ship's ensign in harbour. After this I went to the ship's cinema and saw a film called "Berlin Hotel".

To wind up an excellent day we had a ship's concert. After all the excitement of Christmas Day, Boxing day was treated as a normal day as far as ship's duties was concerned because the ship was to set sail once again on it's journey home. We left Aden harbour at eight o'clock in the morning and passed the cruiser "Devonshire" and the aircraft carrier "Victorious".

Admiral Power addressed the ship's company for the first time the following morning saying that he was sure we were all looking forward to going home and back into "Civvy Street" once again. Our speed today was only 18 knots. Because of economy the average daily speeds were low, although we were still nearing the Suez Canal we were preparing the ship for her arrival in Portsmouth. This meant that the ship had to be cleaned and painted in order to look presentable on arrival in home waters. The signal section had the job of painting the flag deck. Also at this particular time in readiness for our arrival, all foreign currencies had to changed into English money.

It was now the 29th December 1945 and we had arrived at Port Taufiq which is the entrance to the Suez Canal. Sailing slowly through the canal we reached the Bitter Lakes, which is one of the widest parts of the canal, by tea time, here we duly dropped anchor. We only stayed overnight and weighed anchor the following morning, and proceeded along the canal towards Port Said arriving at 4.30 p.m. I went ashore and bought some toy rabbits for the family. There was more painting of the ship's side at Port Said. Being a battleship there was a marine band on board and, at most of the big ports of call on leaving harbour, the band would play the usual nautical tunes, the favourite being of course "Rule Britannia". The next day was New Year's Eve I stayed aboard and did not go ashore. We weighed anchor again the next day proceeding along the Mediterranean on our way to Gibraltar. By now all the ship's company were very much looking forward to reaching the Ship's home port which was Portsmouth, and, incidentally my base.

There was a touch of sadness occurred a few days after leaving Port Said. One of the seamen had a birthday and it was traditional in the navy that when a birthday is celebrated the mess mates usually offer part of their rum ration to the person celebrating. In this case the mess was quite a large one, because of the extra personnel on board, and the seaman had far too much to drink. He decided to sleep it off in one of the ship's 14 inch gun turrets. Unfortunately he fell down to the bottom of the turret pit and later died from his injuries. It was indeed very sad for his family, particularly in view of the fact that he was on his way home after serving abroad. He was duly buried at sea the following day.

The usual watches came along each day. The weather in the Mediterranean was very calm and after a further two days we passed the island of Malta in the distance; then we knew that we were only a few days sailing from Gibraltar. Whilst off duty our favourite pastime was exercising on the upper deck, it was very pleasant, particularly at night in the cool weather. One of the striking differences between conditions now and those during the war which we noticed in the navy was that now all the ports and towns that we visited were all lit up at night whereas before they were in darkness. Neutral countries of course had no need to black out their lights at night.

We were now approaching our last port of call before reaching the United Kingdom. The port was of course Gibraltar, the island famous for its apes. We duly arrived and although shore leave was allowed, I did not go ashore. We only spent 24 hours in the port and we were once again under way. This time the marine band played the ship out of harbour for the final time with a number of tunes which was very moving. On leaving Gibraltar our next stretch of water was the famous Bay of Biscay.

Once again the Bay lived up to it's reputation of providing heavy seas. This brought the usual ban on the forecastle because the sea was splashing over it, and we did not want any more casualties on our last stage of our voyage home. After a while we had calmer weather conditions although we were still in the middle of winter and in January 1946.

It was now time to get ourselves and the ship ready for reaching our final destination; Portsmouth harbour. The battleship Howe was to be "paid off", in other words this was the end of this particular mission. When a ship nears harbour it is decorated with flags and bunting from the forecastle to the stern and in addition a long white pendant is flown from the masthead. On entering the harbour, the whole of H.M.S. Howe's crew were lined up on various parts of the ship. I was stationed on the forecastle. The moment had arrived when the battleship H.M.S. Howe slowly eased it's way into Portsmouth harbour and finally came to a halt after a very long and interesting journey from Singapore. It was a memorable occasion with the band playing and hundreds of people at the dock side waiting to greet their loved ones. Of course Movietone News cameras were there to record the event. About two weeks later I visited the local cinema and saw the news reel of the Howe entering harbour, unfortunately the cameras had concentrated on the bridge of the ship and I had been on the forecastle. Never mind, it was good to see this great battleship on film.

So ended one of the most interesting and adventurous parts of my short career in the Royal Navy; after just two years and two months service. The next objective was to get all my luggage, kit bag, etc., off the ship and report to the depot at Portsmouth prior to attending at the special demobilisation centre set up at the base. On arrival we handed in our service uniforms and in return we were fitted out with civilian clothes ready to become a civilian once again. Before being fitted out with our clothing we were given a lecture on what to expect when one returned to civilian life; things would be quite different to the days before the war. Under a new government directive, for those service personnel who were employed before going into the services, their former employers were obliged to provide jobs on their return. In my case my former employer, an accountant, was still in business but only in a small way and only employed one clerk, and so I decided to look elsewhere for employment. Fortunately, after a holiday of three to four weeks enjoying the freedom after so many years in the services, I was able to find employment with a firm of Chartered Accountants.

The first member of our family to be demobilised had been my brother Frank, he had served in the R.A.F. during the war as a fitter on the ground staff; he saw service overseas in Northern Rhodesia in South Africa. My sister Doreen had been the next to leave the forces, she had served in the A.T.S. in this country and Northern Ireland. I was the last to return to "civvy street" in January 1946.

Medals and Awards.

The medals awarded by His Majesty's Government after the Second World War for my participation were as follows;-

1. The 1939-45 Star

2. The Italy Star

3. The Defence Medal

4. The War Medal 1939-45

Whilst serving with the Kings Own Yorkshire Light Infantry on the 14th February 1943, I was awarded a three year Service and Good Conduct Stripe.

War Medals
From left to right;
The Defence Medal, The 1939-45 War Medal, The Italy Star,
The 1939 - 45 Star.

Notes: -

(1) It was decided 50 years after the war by the Maltese Government to strike a war medal for all service men and women who had served in Malta during the period 1940 to 1943. I served in the Maltese naval base of H.M.S. St. Angelo in 1944 and therefore I did not qualify for the medal.

(2) In 1993, an attempt was made by an individual who had served in Malaya, a Mr. P. Dawson of Keyworth, Nottingham, to persuade the Malaysian Government to strike a war medal for all service men and women who had seen service in Malaysia. However six years on nothing has come of the proposal so far.

Chapter 19.

Aftermath of World Conflicts.

Since the end of the Second World War, various conflicts have taken place between rival parties. The Gulf War, The Falklands War, unrest in Bosnia, in addition to civil wars within a number of African countries.

It would appear that countries do not seem to learn lessons from previous conflicts, although human beings generally whatever nationality seem to be unable to agree amongst themselves. It was usually a question of individuals wanting power both in the First World War with Kaiser William of Germany, and in the Second World War, with German Corporal Hitler of World War One who decided that it would be a good idea to gain revenge against the British because of the suffering of the German people as a result of the conditions set down in the Treaty of Versailles at the end of World War One. After all they started the war and caused wholesale slaughter and suffering.

At the end of World War One, Armistice Day the 11th November 1918 was observed as a day of remembrance in the years that followed, with a two minutes silence on that day at eleven o'clock each morning. Also special services of thanksgiving were held to remind people of the horrors of war. This practice continued until the beginning of the Second World War. During the period between the two world wars, the two minutes silence was strictly observed, no matter what you were doing, every one, individuals, transport, buses and trains, etc., stopped for the two minutes silence.

I was born just a year after the end of the First World War and I remember as a child attending an Armistice Day church service of remembrance in the Patrington church, known as the King of the Holderness. With regard to the two minutes silence I remember when I was at school, whilst playing on the school playing fields, the football matches were stopped for the two minutes silence.

Since the fiftieth anniversary of the end of World War Two, interest in the last two world wars has increased, and more and more people, in particular the younger generation are beginning to learn how the ordinary civilians suffered as well as the armed forces during the two world wars.

We now have in place the United Nations Assembly which consists of delegates from most countries throughout the World. We had the League of Nations after the First World War, but it was not a success because many nations withdrew from the organisation a few years after the League was set up. Now, however, the United Nations Assembly has more "Bite" and seems to be working very well. At the moment we have conflicts between some of the new nations within South Africa, and in these cases of high population, the civilians seem to suffer very badly and are the innocent victims of unnecessary conflicts.

Today's disputes seem to arise within nations because a certain group of individuals or assemblies wish to assert their power over the existing governments, rather like some noisy neighbours or nuisances we all seem to experience these days.

We must not forget the Vietnam conflict between North and South in the 1960s in which the United States of America lost thousands of men in an effort to solve the problem between the two sides. Another good example of differences within certain groups and parties is the Northern Ireland problem. This has been going on for several decades, the question of Northern Ireland and the Irish mainland. Since 1929 when the British Government declared Northern Ireland a separate state and, being part of the United Kingdom, certain groups have opposed the arrangement with violence and killings. At the time of writing (1998) a cease fire is in place and negotiations have now taken place between the Irish Government, The British Government and the different parties in Northern Ireland. The latest development is that a referendum is to be held in May 1998 on proposals for a peace settlement drawn up by all the various parties; we shall await the outcome of the vote, which will be a yes or no.

Part 3. My Father's War Memories

Chapter 21.

My Father's participation in World War 1. 1914 - 1918.

The following were some notes I found in the papers of my late father, who died in 1982. They are about his experiences in the First World War. These were his exact words as used in the notes.

This is in no way just an account of experiences in the 1914-18 war. It is an account of how providence, or fate, if you like, protected me. It all started on a Bank Holiday in August 1914. I was at home then (Newstead Street) for a few days as I was working in Scunthorpe. My pals there wrote to me and said they were joining up, would I go with them? I told my father that I intended to join them and went off to my boarding house in Scunthorpe. When I arrived, my landlady told me that her next door neighbour desired a word with me (he was a manager at Lysaghts Steel Works). He offered me a job there which was more money and less hours than my present job. I took the job, and so I did not join up untill 1915.

After finishing my infantry training in the East Yorkshire Regiment at Dalton, East Yorks. I was sent off on a course to learn machine gunnery - this was north of Newcastle. I mastered the intricacies of this machine and all that remained before passing out was to fire a course on the range.

Then came a scare of landings on the east coast, so I was sent back to my battalion and we spent the night "standing to" in hurriedly dug trenches on the sea front. Since I was not a qualified machine gunner, I was detailed off to join the signallers, and so it was not until 1917 that I was sent to France (This was on my birthday, 28th June 1917).

The following episodes are not in any date order. In March 1918, the Germans broke through our lines and our battalion was rushed into new positions, but I was not with them.

I had been sent to battalion headquarters to help to stack all the goods that was being left behind; canteen stores, blankets, equipment,

My Father
Dressed in his army uniform and
taken during the 1914 - 18 war.

etc. It had been hastily stored in the barn of a farmhouse. Owing to
a misunderstanding between the sergeant major and the battalion
quarter master sergeant, I was left behind with a corporal to keep an
eye on these stores, so I missed that action.

   In April 1918 there was another break-through by the Germans
and we were rushed off to the line in old buses. We were again in a
hastily dug trench and we saw the Germans advancing before we
took up our positions. Two sergeants debated which one of them
should be in charge of the signallers. The loser went off to one end
of the trench and I was with the other. We saw the Germans assemble
a field gun and fire it. The shell fell into our trench where this other

Sergeant was and of course there were casualties. Some men jumped out of the trench and tried to run back on to a road, but not all of them made it.

Finally the sergeant in charge said that if any one cared to risk it, they had better go as the Germans were skulking behind a hedge and were opening fire with machine guns. I took the chance and raced across the open, avoiding bodies of others who had tried in vain. Those remaining in the trench were taken prisoner.

Coming to a gateway, I was met by an officer waiving his revolver and threatening to shoot me for, as he said, "retreating in the face of the enemy." However he calmed down and we duly retreated. There was nothing orderly about it, just hundreds of stragglers going down one road. A German plane machine gunned us and I rolled into the side of a ditch by the road.

Eventually I was attached to a Canadian officer and I was told that I was to be a runner. Two of us signallers were detailed off to take messages to the Canadians (that is if we could find them), there was to be about a fifty-yard interval between us. At one place we had to go down on hands and knees since machine gun bullets were flying over us. The runner in front had stopped, he did not know which way to go. I caught up with him and we eventually saw the Canadians in a trench. When we got near to the trench an officer jumped out and came to us to find out why we were wandering about. Just then a shell dropped a few yards away. Two soldiers were injured and went off on stretchers. I was blown a few yards and later on found a large piece of shrapnel had embedded itself in my haversack. My reading books in my haversack had probably saved my life. I was deaf for a few hours. I had been out repairing telephone wires and when I returned to the trench, the others had finished their tea. So I crawled into the "bivvy" (a slot in the side of the trench with room to just sit up in and to lie down) I had just started my tea, when a shell dropped into the trench. My friend who was at the front of my "bivvy" was killed instantly, six others were also killed and the rest wounded. I was the only one not touched.

A raid was planned to get hold of some German prisoners. I was chosen to go on it, and we had maps to study and the plan of the attack. Then came the day and the attack was to be that night. I am reading in my "bivvy", when I heard my name called. I had to collect my gear and go to battalion headquarters and off to England on leave, so I missed the attack to obtain some German prisoners.

At one time, I was sent off with other "old sweats" for a few days rest on the French coast. We lived in tents and could see the white cliffs of Dover. When we returned to our unit we found they had been in action and suffered heavy casualties.

THE END

Acknowledgement of Photographs.

The photographs featured in Part 1, The Army Years, are all reproductions, with a few exceptions, of family photographs taken mainly by my father during the war. With regard to Part 2, The Royal Navy, the majority of the photographs were originally taken by the yeoman of signals aboard the L.S.T. 3033. He was given permission to take them by the captain of the ship. He used an ordinary every day camera which produced very small picture sizes, approximately two inches by one and a half inches. Some were even smaller. The yeoman did his own developing and was able to make copies available for the ships company who were interested. I was able to obtain between 15 or 20 various photographs, some of which I have used in this biography. My son Martin was responsible for reproducing all the photographs. He is a first class amateur photographer and is a member of Doncaster's T.T.L. Camera Club; my thanks go to him for his interest and time devoted to this work. It is all the more remarkable when you realise that the original photographs were taken between fifty-three to fifty-five years ago. Most importantly they add to the authenticity of the memoirs and thus make it much more interesting and valuable.

Martin Litchfield